The Care and Feeding of FREEDOM

Reclaiming Our Destiny in a World of Confusion

RONALD E. SPRINGER

ISBN: 978-0-9976483-0-0

Library of Congress Control Number: 2016908657

First Published by Bulldozer Press on July 4, 2016
Detroit, Michigan

First Printed in the United States of America
North Charleston, South Carolina

*Special thanks to sculptor James Muir for bringing Lady Justice to life.

"We hold these truths to be self-evident, that all men are created equal, that they are endowed by their Creator with certain unalienable Rights, which among these are Life, Liberty and the pursuit of Happiness.

Whenever any Form of Government becomes destructive of these ends, it is the Right of the People to alter or to abolish it, and to institute new Government, laying its foundation on such principles and organizing its powers in such form, as to them shall seem most likely to affect their Safety and Happiness.

Governments long established should not be changed for light and transient causes; but when a long train of abuses and usurpations, pursuing...a design to reduce them under absolute Despotism, it is their right, it is their duty, to throw off such Government, and to provide new Guards for their future security."

The Declaration of Independence, July 4th, 1776

Table of Contents

Chapter One

Our *Second* Declaration of Independence

A spectre is haunting America—the spectre of a fear so devastating it has shaken the core of our Republic. Desperation has engulfed those not deserving to suffer; our hope lies captive beneath a mask still worn by the guilty. But the shell of immorality that has encrusted our nation is crumbling; it has exposed what the most corrupt never wanted us to see. It is time to declare our convictions independent of those who would secure our silence. Instead of replacing our government, we must return to our founding principles, but with a fresh new moral perspective, and remove from control those who've brought the weight of ruin upon us. Two elements are paramount to this end:

That Americans rise and show the world what they stand for as a people, and perhaps as important, what they *don't* stand for.

That the American people awaken to a new level of moral clarity—an organic moral view we can all agree on—for the proper, harmonic guidance of our lives, our relationships, and our country.

A DECLARATION OF MORAL INDEPENDENCE FROM THE TRAUMAS WEIGHING ON OUR NATION

"When they no longer believe, they can be made to believe by force." —Niccolo Machiavelli

1. For dubious terror attacks against the citizens of the United States and other countries, committing mass murder and property devastation.
2. For carrying out unnecessary wars in pursuit of morally questionable ideals.
3. For corrupting the American Monetary System, resulting in a new depression which if left unchecked, could spiral us into a new dark age.
4. For irresponsible lending oversight that has resulted in the foreclosure of millions of homes.
5. For permitting the destruction of American industry through unfair trade agreements.
6. For permitting our infrastructure to crumble, causing peril and exacerbating our economic crisis.
7. For permitting executives to strip companies of working capital as "compensation" with no personal liability, causing mass layoffs, and leaving enterprises overly vulnerable to adverse conditions.
8. For polluting our air, water, and food with toxic, life-threatening chemicals.
9. For denying our citizens the best health care treatments in favor of special interest profitability.

10. For the unprecedented growth of secret intelligence services not subject to public laws, oversight, or accountability.
11. For undermining and toppling democratically-elected governments around the world.
12. For performing coups through rigged elections and assassination, at home and abroad.
13. For ignoring our laws, overriding our constitutional protections and subjecting people to imprisonment without charge, violation of privacy, censorship, and torture.
14. For corrupting the press with financial rewards or threats of dismissal, suppressing evidence of wrongdoing, and discouraging popular discussion.

Such actions amount to high treason against America and all of humanity, many of which we have struggled with since our country's inception. The intent is to remove our freedoms and weaken us so that we cannot resist complete hegemonic domination, in violation of the First, Fourth, Fifth, Sixth, Eighth, Ninth, and Tenth Amendments of our Constitution. It is time for one final changing of the guard. To accomplish this requires that we empower the people like never before, and that means a reevaluation of all we consider moral and good, as Americans and as world citizens dedicated to liberty and justice for all.

Our *Second* Declaration of Independence

"I'd rather die a broken piece of jade, than live a life of clay."
—Bruce Lee

College tuition didn't used to bankrupt Americans. Neither did health care. Neither did divorce. These key aspects of life have become the focal point of mass control for the well-financed evils in our society. If you want to better yourself, you face a financial gauntlet. If you get sick or injured, your bills will now accelerate you into bankruptcy in three days. If you fall in love and it doesn't work out (and half of all marriages fail), you will be financially devastated. Instead of fostering our dreams of success, safety, and romantic fulfillment, these core American values now promote fear, tremendous risk, and alarm in us all. Our deepest, most sacred values are literally being held for ransom. Our pursuit of life, liberty, and happiness now suffers a tax that has all but reversed the intent of our revolution. Why?

The thieving rich in America have done what the likeminded throughout history have always done. They have placed anchors around the necks of the classes below them, retarding any effort we make to aspire to the upper classes. They have set up the system so their dominance will never be challenged, and we are now paying dearly for it.

"Distinctions in society will always exist under every just government. Equality of talents, of education, or of wealth cannot be produced by human institutions...every man is equally entitled to protection by law; but when the laws undertake to add

to these natural and just advantages artificial distinctions, to grant titles, gratuities, and exclusive privileges, ... the humble members of society – the farmers, mechanics, and laborers – who have neither the time nor the means of securing like favors for themselves, have a right to complain of the injustice of their government. There are no necessary evils in government. Its evils exist only in its abuses. If it would confine itself to equal protection, and, as heaven does its rains, shower its favor alike on the high and the low, the rich and the poor, it would be an unqualified blessing."

—President Andrew Jackson

While President Jackson's quote is critical of bad government, it applies *universally* to the struggle between decent and indecent people, and *that* is what this book is about. The fact is that all throughout history, a certain type of man has been responsible for society's traumas, and the good news is his actions are *very* predictable. To understand them, we have to take a step back and witness a war that has raged on, practically unnoticed for centuries; a war we never knew we were fighting.

The most honorable people—those of innocent motive and dedicated labor—have always seen their ultimate goals frustrated by their inability to understand or express the moral foundation of their actions. The rug gets pulled primarily by the inversion of moral principles within *their own* minds. Second, by the moral subversion inflicted by others, and third by the simple absence of knowledge on critical social issues affecting every one of us. The unfortunate consequence is that the tools of mass prosperity can be turned against mankind with the power of moral uncertainty, and used for mass murder. They can and they have, repeatedly, throughout history. Look what had to be accepted in order for Germany to take the course it did in Nazi times. Conversely, look what had to be accepted in order for America to be born. These great surges were driven by the moral philosophy accepted by the masses. When the prominent in society built on Aristotle and Thomas Paine, the result was America. When they built on Kant and Nietzsche, the result was the horrors of The Third Reich. When they built on Hegel and Marx, the result was a very bloody Soviet Russia.

Moral philosophy is the fundamental driver of mankind. It determines every action we take and gets more sensitive as men make decisions together. We are at a juncture in human history where we must reevaluate and reaffirm what we consider moral. It is time for a new philosophy, or if you prefer, one that links us back to the principles that founded America, and advances them in a super-modern way. The need is obvious: the world is suffering from a plethora of *moral confusion*. Regardless of the morality we have been brought up under—be it Christian or otherwise—what we hoped to learn from childhood on was a *format for living* acknowledged by all as correct, so that we could feel good about our actions in life and become the best person we could be. What we encountered instead was a lot of confusing and contradictory beliefs resulting in massive disunity, while we expected our moral code to give us confidence, peace of mind, and to bring people together. How could this be?

We live in the most advanced society the world has ever known. We have launched ourselves into outer space and have harnessed the atom; yet we still hesitate in uncertainty over the declaration of every moral step! Actually, good and evil are so intertwined in our culture that neither is independently recognizable. This plague has caused a nightmare of infighting the world over, between and among every sect, every faith and even among those who wish to be left out of it. It is time for it to end.

I am here to say that *there is* a crystal clear, non-contradictory structure for morality, and it is based on nature itself. The structure follows our pattern of cognition, and as the purpose of cognition is life, it reveals the structure of evil as well—in any break with the moral pattern. This natural process is the basis for sound mental health, sound relationships, and provides the structure for mankind's proper organizations. It governs and can be seen in *all* human action.

We all know that *moral* is the proper way to be, but the way it is preached, morality is often the very thing we need protection *from*. Why? It is because that certain type of men have been riding and torturing the rest through an inverted moral code, where the good is the evil and the evil is the good; a weapon most people have never conceived of or thought to question. I'm going to free you from their grasp and show you the kind of world we deserve.

Do you ever wonder if you are good enough? Morally-certain people don't have to wonder. Think you are a coward for being afraid of life sometimes? It is time to find out what cowardice *really* is. Actually, there is so much right about our personal and social actions in this world, that we have very little to fear in the way of negative self-discovery. The guilt in our lives is mostly unjustified, and many problems we feel looming up behind us aren't even there. If you can comprehend these words, there is nothing fundamentally wrong with you! For most of mankind, moral confusion is like walking out of the house with messed up hair. Nothing is essentially missing; it is just humorously unkempt and needs to be straightened out. The wonderful discovery you are in for, is finding out just how much of what you have done for *your own* prosperity is directly in line with the moral progress of mankind; that most of your actions have been natural, and *right.* And just as important is how to identify and correct if necessary, the premises driving the other aspects of your existence, so that all of your motives flow together in one common, life-furthering direction.

Chapter Two

Is A Perfect World Even Possible?

"Take from life what is pure, and for living, what is sufficient."
—Arabian proverb

Most of us picture the ideal life as living in harmony with the flow of nature itself; where you would tap into its grace and be as one with the universe, and I agree, but that is not the *only* view.

Let's talk about our perfect world. What is it? Most often we would hear *"Heaven on Earth"* Where no one has to work, food drops into our mouths for the price of opening it, and rivers flow with milk and honey. The problem is, as this defies nature and we wouldn't be earning the products that can only be created by others, we would have to seize them. Whenever a civilization has attempted to realize such a heaven on Earth, a slave society has emerged.

Here is my version of a perfect world. I wake up to sunshine and the birds are singing. I suds-about in the tub and get squeaky clean. I select some dapper threads and spend some quality time checking myself out in the mirror. *I never get sick of it...* Then I grab my briefcase, kiss the wife and 2.5 kids and head out to the garage. Awaiting me is my dream car; a Ferrari or a Lamborghini, and it was no lottery prize; I earned it. It's mine. I lay two patches twenty feet long and it's off to my dream job.

I'm not rude to people in traffic. Flow is everything, so I anticipate their actions and help them get in the flow or out of it if I can. Driving is an adventure; there are no horns blaring because most of us are enjoying ourselves out there, and we are patient when we should be. As far as I'm concerned, every old lady is *my* grandmother. Cops aren't out there slowing things down, ticketing people for speeding. Again, flow is everything. They ticket only those whose conduct is disruptive.

I'm headed to a place where I *want* to be. I work with people I genuinely like and look forward to seeing. We have come together to create and offer products that benefit others and allow us to live the kind of lives we want to live. There is certainly pressure to perform in our work, but it is *productive* tension that makes us feel good about ourselves, and makes others value us even more because we handle it so well. They pay me well; they know they have to. We work a full day but know when to call it quits. Many of us have a romantic evening ahead.

The one I chose to spend my life with is on my mind. She is my greatest achievement, and I reflect on that accomplishment often, because attaining *all* precious goals are alike in mind. I landed her, and when the going gets tough I think of her, and it is a reconfirmation that I can win my deepest values. If I keep striving and never give up, I can generate all the bounty and happiness I need.

I saw her for the first time and my stomach dropped. I knew I deserved her, but she didn't know it yet. Whatever I said, it worked! And I was able to build the relationship over time. Now she is my greatest fan and I am hers. We stand behind each other 100% to be as fulfilled as possible. She wants me to *be the man* and knows I have to earn it—in my own eyes. I want her to feel appreciated for her feminine power, and for what it does to me. Both of us need to feel desirable and deeply desired; that is why we stay trim and active, and spend our lives on growing.

She is beautiful, and it is not just what nature gave her; it is how she feels about living. The look of exhilaration and adventure is always a part of her expression. As a result, the facial muscles associated to beauty have gotten a real workout over the course of her life. We both feel excited about the new discoveries awaiting us around all of life's corners, so we remain bright and alive. The values we strive for creates a challenge to remain worthy of each other. Other suitors take notice, which constantly emits romantic appeal; so the fire between us has never died.

Our kids look at us with embarrassment and envy; they see what they want for their own futures. They know we have something special between us that is private and exciting. We are in love and it is written all over us. They dream of the enchantment of being endeared to another, which will one day add a whole new dimension to their lives, and they can't wait to grow up and become worthy of it.

Our kids have grown, watching us live productive lives. They see us deal with insincere people sternly to protect our clean, honorable lifestyle and keep the evils out. They see us striving toward goals, and fostering others to do the same. They see our setbacks, our determination, and our triumphs. They see how we spend our leisure time, whether it is skiing in the Alps or sailing down the coast, but it is all based in some way on our own accomplishments. They learn the pattern of success and fulfillment *by example*. They *know* what it takes and absorb our disciplines so they can focus on what *they* want in life, and achieve it.

There are few teen struggles in the family, because there is nothing to rebel against. We as parents understand the growth phases; we know they need to become independent. We didn't shelter them from personal responsibilities, leaving them unprepared for the world. We steadily *increased* their self-responsibility, so they could leave the nest soaring.

Life is running smoothly; relationships are sound; I'm doing what I enjoy. I go to sleep, *excited* about tomorrow.

I don't need a mansion or to control the world to lead what I feel is a near perfect existence. All I need is freedom, and the rest is up to me. This is what is possible to us all by America's founding principles, and I'm thankful that I have been able to live such a fulfilling life for most of my years.

Having enjoyed a self-guided, fantasy lifestyle makes crisis in America all the more alarming. Like most other Americans, my conduct has not been irresponsible. My actions were not goaded by short-term greed or a lack of foresight. I did not bring this nightmare upon myself nor upon my brethren; so why are we the ones suffering?

Centralized control permits centralized mistakes (or evils) to disturb every individual of the nation. One advantage of spreading power among men is the cushion it provides to the errors and immoralities of others. The more control we have over our own lives, the less the decisions of others can do us harm. Our frightening dilemma today is that most of what the Founding Fathers intended has been reversed, so what happens in Washington (or in the secret corridors of power) affects every one of us on a very personal level. Due to this, the American dream is not only at risk, the country itself is in tragic jeopardy.

If you are like me, the perfect world I described is enough for you. Perhaps you would add your own business to the dream, a private jet, a worldwide philanthropic effort, or the desire to be President of the United States one day, but the goals you have chosen are honest and wholesome, as are your methods in their pursuit. I absolutely support you for this, but it isn't a clear road ahead. It is important to know that at the same time, there are those among us who have no regard for anything wholesome whatsoever. The *destruction* of the American dream is their goal. There are those who can (and do) reach so far into the abyss that it is unspeakable even to contemplate; but we *must* be aware of it if we want to preserve our way of life—for ourselves, for our children, and for the generations to follow.

President Obama has mentioned that we are fed many erroneous assumptions and false alternatives such as big vs. small government, when we should be focused on *effective* government. Likewise, our *shades of grey* put a halt to moral judgment, leaving us defenseless. What if we could take the aversion away from discussions of morality and make it effective, too? Let's expose evil for once, and see if they can survive full sunlight. Let's go ahead and realize *their* worst nightmare as well and expose *the good,* so that we are not at the mercy of a new leader every four years. Let's establish *a leader in every life.*

Chapter Three

The Mindset Responsible for Our Freedom

The actual purpose of morality has always been awry. Morality doesn't start with a kind smile, a shared seat, or anything between men. It is *not* primarily social. It begins alone, in our relationship to existence itself. When morality is adjusted to its proper intention, everything else in life falls right into place. Morality is not something you give homage to for a few hours on Sunday, then forget about while you are busy making a living. Morality is the *means* by which you pursue the action of living. People know implicitly what is moral and immoral. Nature tells them. Other's reactions tell them. It is not difficult to evaluate what furthers the life of a man or what hinders it; as it is not difficult to ascertain that sustaining organic life *is* the main issue of morality.

The True Moral Division between Men

From the dawn of time, mankind has been in a class war; not between rich and poor, white and black, or weak and strong, but between rational motive and irrational motive; between dependence and independence; between Fear-driven Man and Self-made Man. These are the true moral divisions of mankind; fear on one side, anticipation on the other. At one's first moment of conscious awareness, one sees the world, and is either afraid of its complexity or is intrigued. One either immediately desires exploration or tries to back out. This initial reaction sets the stage for the manner in which one's mind will classify information or assimilate, from then on. The question truly is, "To be, or not to be," and from the very beginning of cognitive responsibility, Self-made Man decides that he wants to live. Fear-driven Man wants something very different.

The Pattern of Cognition

Moral awareness begins with the recognition of our natural thought pattern, a discovery I have found to be identical for everyone, contrary to popular belief. All men require the same nutrients to survive. The needs of water and oxygen are *axiomatic,* or in other words, are self-evident, foundational truths. Axiomatic needs are fundamentally irrefutable and reach substantially deeper than most imagine. They transcend the physical needs of sunlight, water and air to reveal links directly into conceptual processes.

Every man's mind classifies information alike, building concepts in a four-step pattern, and we either reject this natural design, or learn to act in accordance with it. Its first step is *perception,* the open integration of clear, coherent sensory data. We *begin* life and every day thereafter absorbing what we hear, see, smell and feel, and then we move on to determine what our senses are picking up. This second step is *identification,* the act of distinguishing the objects of our perceptions, their attributes, and the specific relevance and value they have to us. Proper integration of this data builds our knowledge of the world into a non-contradictory whole, from which sound choices can be made. *Reason* is the process of making those sound choices, reflecting off this base to establish plans for the third step, *productive action.* The fourth and final step is the product of all that has come before; the *result.* For Self-made Men, most often the result is a reward, a beneficial outcome achieved by intention, such as a positive emotional state, a thought-provoking observation, a paycheck, or the United States of America.

Reward can be mistaken to be *only* a resultant factor, not a part of the process. Reward is not an element separate from cognition—not an isolated result that can be stolen or divided in any way from that which it was borne—but contains vital information about the soundness of our thought process and determines our steadfastness of course. Another word for *result* in this process is *validation.*

Of course, the fundamental reward of all living creatures practicing the pattern consistently, is life itself.

The pattern is simple:

1) Perception,
2) Identification,
3) Creative Action, and
4) Reward.

We see what we want, we identify the means, we take action and we get a result. All human action follows this pattern, from applying the brakes of a car to getting a drink of water to running a business, and a Self-made Man will be able to recall enough instances in his past to see the pattern operating at all levels implicitly. We all run this process in everything we do, all day long, every day of our lives. Test it. For example, 1) you feel dryness in your mouth; 2) you identify it as thirst; 3) you head to the drinking fountain, 4) you quench it. Another example: 1) you see the car in front of you slowing down; 2) you identify it as a danger; 3) you press the brakes; 4) no accident: life's flow continues uninterrupted.

Perception, identification, creative action, and reward: this is the pattern of life. You could describe it in many more steps if you wanted to, but simplicity is key to usefulness. See for yourself in any instance: stay aware of the steps; pace what physically happens within you, and in time, you will come to recognize the pattern clearly, and develop a quick confidence in your every action. With practical awareness of it in daily life, it will become the foundation of a spectacular moral power that you will able to harness in short order. The moral aspect of this pattern is that it is thee life-furthering guide for Man—an abstract description of thought which parallels the biological process—and every step is optional, though the consequences of their evasion are not. A man must accept life as his standard of value—as his basic referent—by choice, and the four steps of perception, identification, creative action, and reward show the fundamental life-pattern—the definitive moral dynamic of a human being.

You may ask, What about instincts? Human beings don't have any. Our reflexes might be able to pull away from a hot stove, but they can't direct us to build a house, plant a garden or guide an enterprise. We are entirely self-guided. Our perceptions likewise, give us no automatic course of action. In order to survive we must make choices. In order to validate our choices, we must accept a standard of value by which to weigh them, and the standard for Man and all living things is the alternative of life or death. This is the bridge between us all: the universal purpose of morality itself. Whatever protects and furthers life is the good; whatever hinders or destroys it, is the evil. The conscious choice of life-serving action is our key moral choice. Steering a car, crossing a street, selecting groceries, pursuing a career—these are all decisions originating through sensate perception, which begins a cognitive process of reflecting on what will further our lives versus what will take it from us.

As we have no instincts to guide us, proper cognition is the abstract necessity of life for Man. It isn't a separate issue from our need of air and water, but an extension of the same requirement. The whole structure of consciousness is meant to protect us; from the need of clarity and confidence, to the stable environment we achieve through our work, to the pride we feel by doing it right. Cause and effect can be identified from one end of it to the other. The purpose of this cause-and-effect relationship is to produce confidence—a necessity for a non-instinct driven consciousness—which acts as a constant barometer of our physical and spiritual well-being. Confidence attained is never a fixed state, is it? It can vary from brimming to anemic, just as our situations vary. Not only that, confidence needs replenishing even more frequently than the body needs food (imagine if every right turn was supposed to be a left!). We hear that pride is evil, but pride or self-esteem, is simply our awareness that the majority of our actions are correct; a reward we have to earn every day (and practically every moment), and which we could not live without. The closer we get to practicing the structures nature intended, the healthier we are psychologically.

This pattern goes on and will go on, with our without your awareness of it. If you take control of the pattern, you can have complete moral certainty, and all of its rewards on demand. Morality is not primarily social. It begins alone, in our relation to existence itself. Our first moral obligation is to achieve independence; we have to be competent enough to sustain ourselves. In the social realm, we just have to do it in a civil way. It's that simple.

So what kind of man has historically followed this pattern? We watch cable specials about Napoleon, Gangues Khan and Pope John Paul, but centuries later, do we benefit from their existence? On the other hand, we move through rooms turning lights on and off, we drive our cars to work every day, we wear nice clothes and we fly to vacation and business destinations. These are all products of another type of man—Thomas Edison, Henry Ford, Eli Whitney, and the Wright Brothers. Isn't there an essential difference in the quality of their contribution? They say but for a handful of men over the course of human existence, none of civilization would have been possible. The vantage point of morality in action is often as witness to the pioneers of our past and present. By following the structure of their course, we can define the motives, means and ends of the actual good. To the limits of their vision, they create and further our great industries and set the best examples for the whole world to follow. These are the men of purpose. With their every moment drenched in meaning as a result, they are the happiest, deepest, most devoted, and most genuine people on Earth. Self-made men are those who utilize the human mind as it was meant to be, and can show the rest how to actualize their greatest potential. Our appreciation for these men is our respect for life itself, as the natural reason for purpose *is* life.

A Sound Individual: Self-made Man

Perception

Nature provides an advantage to every living species, making it possible for all to sustain and perpetuate life. We watch the Discovery Channel in awe of the keen eyesight of the owl and the hawk, the agility of the cheetah, the shark's acute sense of smell—senses and abilities that give every animal an edge in its survival. We don't have to question their value. We know that the sharper the senses are for an animal, the more powerful its capacity to feed and protect itself, and this is true for Man as well. Nature adorned *us* with the largest creative brain-mass, many times the size of our nearest biological relative, empowering us with immense control over our consciousness. Self-made Man looks at the world alone. In his world, men *can* see, hear, and comprehend. Walking into a wall with his eyes closed is all the proof he needs to validate the importance of his senses. He knows that the clarity of his perception determines the quality of his life. To depend on others at any fundamental level is intolerable, flying in the face of his struggle to become a self-sufficient adult.

Self-made Man doesn't question his capacity to think, to feel, to sense or to live. He knows he can, and his highest judge is himself. He makes up his own mind what makes sense and what doesn't, who is honest and who isn't, and gets to the bottom of any issue with the clearest chain of knowledge necessary to act. He spends his time serving, creating, and defending his own life and its peaceful progression. He inherently knows what is good for him or evil. He doesn't tolerate the idiocy that demands the subordination of his sensibilities. He doesn't accept irrational premises that cannot be validated in the course of his own existence. He does not allow assertions to replace his perceptions. He moves at his own comfortable pace, veering only when necessary to avoid or stamp out whoever claims a dogmatic right to bar his way.

With the incredible level of data collected in the medical and physical sciences, we have more than enough evidence to develop a sound moral philosophy for Man. So many human attributes considered evil have been proven to be biologically natural, life-promoting structures, that the false-righteously stiff sit frozen as their control over morality is taken. Their stranglehold on innocence is succumbing to age, finally. Why did they fight rationality? The concepts of judgment, certainty, and pleasure, which were considered impertinent, arrogant, and selfish, have proven themselves to be derived by axiomatic needs—basic needs for the *conscious* health of Man—just as air and water are necessities of physical health. *Judgment* is the identification and acceptance of right and wrong; *certainty* is the established link of cause to effect, and *pleasure* is the reward for acting on the certainty of rational judgment. Our sexual drives, our emotional propensity for constructive or destructive action, our degrees of intelligence; these are issues that as far as moral import is concerned, can be put to rest. There was and is, no mind/body dichotomy. There is no moral struggle of one against the other. There are no 'I can't help it' actions *without* motive. There is no struggle for control between the conscious and subconscious mind. The struggle is and always has been, between reality and the Fear-driven's unwillingness to accept it.

Everyone feels uncertainty about the unknown until its nature becomes clear. Self-worth is *not* a question of feeling fear or not; that does not define our bravery or our value as a person. What defines our value is how we respond. Some shrink according to their self-belief; Self-made Man expands according to his. But where does his self-confidence come from? It comes from his pattern of thought. The pattern repeats, and while the accumulation of knowledge may be spontaneous and haphazard, the resulting order is not. The new is the unexplored; the startling is the adventurous and he anticipates his own triumph against any challenge.

The Tree of Knowledge (Identification)

Most believe that every mind creates its own reality, that every branch of life has its own tree, and then it is too overwhelming a task to investigate them all. But how much simpler would it be if all branches led to the same trunk?

All sound concepts begin grounded in the axioms of existence itself, and consciousness as the faculty of perceiving existence. These concepts are not different for individual people. We all use the same dictionaries as they all condense data about the same world. As all limbs of a tree are of similar form, so grows our mental structure and the information it contains—branching in the pattern of genus and differentia. If you zoom in, you'll notice that one branch is medicine, while another might be plumbing. Zoom in even closer and you'll see a detailed account of a limb or of the circulatory system—how it works, what helps or hinders it and how we repair its internal and external maladies. Zoom in on the other, and its branches reveal the technical intricacies on the space shuttle, in complex machinery, in our homes, businesses, cars, and hospitals. All branches of knowledge as all branches of a tree, live dependent on their trunk, and any separation means death for the limb. It is the trunk, which is rooted in the ground—that gathers nutrition and provides the living energy to expand and reach new heights. In other words, any disconnection from existence invalidates a concept.

Healthy, valid concepts all serve the same ultimate purpose—providing data upon which men can act. Each branch is held and furthered by the men who harbor that specific interest. There is no central location for the entirety of mankind's knowledge. We all build a knowledge tree, tailored to our own specific interests. The stability and worth of our tree depends on how deeply our roots delve into the soil of existence.

The Role of Emotion

So what part do emotions play in cognition? Emotions ride the torrent of our experience, reading our health, pride, fear, and pain with precision, revealing every situation's significance to us. All emotions are important—good and bad. They indicate the soundness of our course, measuring virtue or vice, reward or penalty.

Self-made Man considers his emotions to be just one of many gauges on his control panel. He does not ignore them, but pays open attention, as to every other measure of health. He traces back through what led him to feel certain emotions in order to continue their causes or to eliminate them.

Monitoring emotional reactions can actually permit you to see into the future. This is something I term Inertial Awareness. Every choice we make immediately generates positive or negative energy; it immediately begins preparing us for the actions to come. Thoughts have momentum; they are preceded and followed by other thoughts, as does physical action.

I work to further the positive inertias in my life. When I make a wrong turn, the inertias stop. It can be *any* choice—the wrong mate, a wrong business affiliation, or the wrong approach. When corrected, the inertias I wish to further are invigorated. Moral consistency is the key to use this kind of awareness to see into your future.

So far we've gone from validating our senses to understanding how we build our tree of knowledge. Now we'll explore the third step of the pattern, *creative action*, which is what we tailor the content of our trees to: our purpose in life.

Purpose (Creative Action)

Purpose can no more be separated from spiritual preservation than profit can be separated from physical preservation. Each is responsible for the other.

At the top of the pyramid, our purpose guides and oversees all integration of data below, sorting what will help or hinder the attainment of our goals. All that lies beneath it is similar for every man—just data—yet without a central purpose, a human being is rudderless. Without it, he floats disconnected to the whole of his life, unable to tell day-to-day, issue-to-issue, what furthers or threatens his long-range goals and desires. We can be swept in any adverse direction by the ceaseless flow of data streaming into our senses if we don't take conscious control. Having lifelong goals, we become aware of the long-range effects of any circumstance, which assures we don't end up in the wrong place.

Thanks to those who've met the needs of civilization, individuals need not make the basic necessities of life their primary concern. Their purpose can exist far along into abstract territory, where an honest living can be made in as many creative ways as there are people.

The men of purpose have a calling; a desire to see some specific end achieved, and the whole of their being is poured into its accomplishment. When they succeed, they find another. They spend their lives on growing, each concern more sophisticated than the one before, as a constant answer to why they live. With their every moment drenched in meaning as a result, they are the happiest, deepest, most devoted, and most genuine people on Earth. Their essential purpose acts as the highest abstraction in their chain of knowledge, and all actions in life and all knowledge accumulated takes place within its framework. As a result, they acquire the longest intellectual range; knowing how every step they take will affect their lives, and are able to project their activities to the end of their days. With their purpose as motivator for every action, no energy is wasted. Their development is streamlined and as a result, their chains of knowledge grow much faster and much longer than usual. These are the men who utilize the mind as it was meant to be, and can show the rest how to actualize their greatest potential.

Now, all men have dreams, but their nature varies in regard to personal integrity. They all include riches and glamour, but his dreams differ from others in that Self-made Man exalts the *effort* necessary to achieve them. He knows that this is the source of his self-worth; not the *having* alone, but the earning. The capacity to *deserve* is the glory of any human being, in wealth, in love, and in honor.

Like most people, I began my career in the pattern of a painful grind and cherished weekends, with torturous years and precious vacations. It was all backwards! Now, when I think of vacation, I think "To escape from what?" I love everything I do.

There is no such thing as forever in human terms. Each second that goes by cannot be recalled, as it is ruthlessly subtracted from the span of our lives. No matter what happens—good or bad—we must enjoy our time here to our fullest capacity. No matter what we accumulate—money, fame, enlightenment—nothing compares to the satisfaction of squeezing every ounce of joy, passion, and adventure out of our conscious hours.

Reward

The fourth cognitive element, the concept of validation, has many faces. The effect of so many causes, it first stands for justice. In this regard, the words *reward* and *consequence* are synonymous. For Self-made Man, it is the glory of his existence. We are the men who see and hear, and trust those perceptions. We are the men who think and feel, and are totally honest about the conclusions we draw and the actions we take. We never, never, *never* drop our minds. We produce and therefore earn the stunning luxuries our freedom makes possible. Beautiful homes, exotic cars, sun-soaked vacations, a life with the mate of our dreams—it is all possible in this land of opportunity. The disciplined focus of our efforts, the intelligent choices and dedicated hours provides a steady climb to heights of our own. We know what we've earned and our work *should be* rewarded, and in America, it is; yet the most important reward is internal. The reward is self-esteem. It is our own sense of justice, knowing our own value and looking outward; ready to accept and give value for value in love and respect for existence and for others; with our greatest human bond reserved for those who live up to our standards. This is *our* spiritual stature.

Happiness

"Some indeed, who start with the opportunity, go wrong from the very beginning of the pursuit of happiness. But as our object is to find the best constitution, and that means the one whereby a state will be best ordered, and since we call that state best ordered in which the possibilities of happiness are greatest, it is clear that we must keep constantly in mind what happiness is. ...Happiness is an activity and a complete utilization of virtue, not conditionally but absolutely." —Aristotle

Most of us recognize the fourth step of validation as happiness. Happiness is not a random, causeless, selfless, indefinable phenomenon relying on mystical or intuitive elements which lie outside our power. **It is a product of the proper thought pattern** practiced by the Self-made: perception, identification, and purposeful action—of all that has come before—and one need only embrace the reality of its pattern. Nature, to be commanded, must be obeyed. Happiness is the *medium* of pride, as pride is the medium of confidence. Each can become a form of wealth. Happiness is an accumulation of positive emotional energy to be enjoyed consciously, as it was borne constructively.

Happiness cannot be had by seeking diversions that clash with our values, or by any means which negate our consciousness, leading nowhere. It cannot be had just by smiling. It cannot be had by serving others. Real, consistent happiness can only be had by those who accept and practice its true foundation. No dead-ends, dependencies, or freebies lead to happiness. It is instead, the radiance of a *fully valued* consciousness. It is a product of achievement. Happiness *is* self-appreciation and can naturally spring from nothing else.

The code of the Self-made brings a man to the point where he is no longer *coping* with existence, but reveling in it. Following his lead, so serene a calm will develop in your control of life that you'll wonder how you ever got along without it. The radiant result of a moral existence as well as its most powerful motivation and product, is a profoundly private, self-fulfilled personal joy.

To develop as happiness, our effort must serve sound, rational goals, but those goals can vary greatly. The desire to bring a new invention into the world, to go where no man has gone before, to close a deal, to be appealing to a certain quality of partner, to turn a faster lap on a racetrack, to express exaltation through art, these are all actions of joy; of pushing oneself to the next level in endeavors self-important to pursue. The joy varies only in degrees according to the personal significance and depth of the endeavor. It is our own passionate interests brought to life in a sound value hierarchy that leads to a consistently earned pride and a deserved happiness. Its depth determines whether the satisfaction is sustainable or fleeting. A surface goal gives off little esteem compared to a long-term goal of greater complexity, but both add to the plus side. The emotional reward for a small accomplishment can last only a few minutes, while the pride of something immense will be much more profound and lasting. Seemingly unrelated, both accumulate as positivism and both serve the same end: a tailor-made existence. If you are interested in a much deeper exploration of what makes a moral individual, *Sovereignty,* my 12 CD set, offers a thorough grounding (available at MoralArmor.com). The result will radiate tremendous goodwill to all those you encounter—our next subject.

Free Your Mind: The Levels beyond Happiness

We've all heard people say, "If I could just be happy..." But Self-made Man doesn't stop there. He sees the road still stretching ahead, so we'll go much further. From the conscious acceptance of existence, to earned confidence, pride and happiness, his next steps, like the others, build on what has come before. From how he deals with stress, to *metaphysical honesty, integrity,* and *rational perfection,* these attributes lead to *intransigence,* and the exalted medium of *full volitional maturity.*

Accepting only what builds a traceable chain of logic, Self-made Man is able to drop all unnecessary cultural stress in a heap. Self-made Man doesn't suffer the mental mix of contradictions where reality is foremost on some issues, but where wishes and nonsense take precedence in others. He doesn't blame himself for circumstances outside of his choice. He doesn't agonize over being out of place, being liked or disliked. He no longer hides his virtue, or frets over his inability to scale the emotional barriers of those unswayed by rationality. Beyond a fundamental respect for civil rights, the idea of conforming *socially* is foreign to him.

By accepting what is possible to change and what isn't, between what is rational and what isn't, all unnecessary conflict within him is eliminated. Knowing that guilt results from a *chosen* evil just as pride results from the *choice* of life-furthering good, he is free to seek the only perfection possible to Man: living in harmony with the flow of life. Doing so, he can see himself openly and accept himself completely.

With the power to define life-furthering values firmly in place, he is able to question all the premises Man ever created, revalidating what works and throwing out what doesn't. The control of others over him is wiped out; the majority of his stress dissipates, and he is free to pursue true integrity. His sophistication soars as his virtues blend into a pattern of lifelong advancement, where all of his deepest human traits are fully utilized. Intransigence adds the weight of experience. He reaches full conviction; not just agreeing with concepts, but *knowing what's right*, through personal validation over time.

There is no greater power for Man than moral certainty. When no oppressive power—inside or outside—is allowed to interrupt your flow, your mental structure takes solid shape and begins to support you in turn. You recover the capacity for action without hesitation. To combine a peaceful inner calm with morally-certain, motive-driven energy is a stunning phenomenon; a feeling of so potent a power for living that you know *this* is the true goal of morality, the very height of personal freedom, and one of the greatest rewards of life.

Chapter Four

The Mindset Responsible for Enslavement

"Irrationality is its own damnation." —Moral Armor

Hell

Often we imagine Hell to be a great cavern of jagged rock and fire—dangerous, but exciting to a higher power just the same; but that is not the true nature of Hell. True Hell doesn't require armor plate to endure, but rubber gloves and clothespins. Hell is immobility, being held back by personal choice, culture, or legislation. Hell is contemplating wonders forever denied to us, dreams never to be reached, happenings that will never happen. Hell is contamination, the infiltration of filth and pestilence allowed to spread uncontested. It is disease left untreated;

disease *welcomed* if you will. Hell is where others dictate your course, yet remain unaccountable. Hell is patiently trying to reason with the unreasonable. Hell is doing 35 MPH when we could be doing eighty. It is the energy of life drained and gone, lethargic eyes too drawn to stay open, and the ill-smelling bum who lacks the common decency to wash.

Hell is seeing our lives consumed: not to serve our highest ability, but to serve that bum. Hell is where high spirit is *not* fostered and *cannot* be sustained. Hell is where the cards are stacked in the favor of evil; where emphasis is placed on alleviating the burdens of stagnation versus protecting the foundations of growth. Not what you expected? No kidding. Hell is where *we* lose.

That of course is Hell from the viewpoint of a Self-made Man, a man of great capacity forced to sit on his energy. But while it limits *us,* it allows another type of man full reign in the use of his capacity. It allows him to posture as leader in place of those who deserve to be. It allows him to invert the *only* sound class structure of Man—sound motive versus unsound motive—and to invert human guidance, taking control away from the most complex thinkers and giving it to the least. Like rats roving over a corpse, it restrains his prey—allowing him to negate cause and effect and to check ability—undermining the best moral minds in favor of those with the lowest immoral aspirations. This Hell exists all around us today, and is *desired* by that type of man. Where does such a man come from? Why does he want to reverse everything? What advantages does he gain?

Fear-driven Man

Being aware of the cognitive process is critical, because when virtue is allowed to pass undefined, then so is vice. With a proper understanding of cognition comes the understanding of *every moral violation,* so now let's look at its poster boy: Fear-driven Man.

Early on, some men suffer a panic attack against the very responsibility of perception and identification. Their terror of self-chosen action is so total that they claw towards any means of its avoidance. Grasping blindly for a substitute driver of their intellect, they turn their senses to the task of securing a stranglehold on those who did not appear to default. From then on, their primary source of judgment and livelihood becomes other men. Upon their first sense of safety, they look out at those who did not fall to the same fear; those capable of experiencing the spiritual rewards of living: pride, satisfaction, love, and happiness. Instead of reverence, they respond with so miserable a hatred that they turn their focus to the task of corrupting every living concept: separating cause from effect, virtue from choice, value from love, productivity from pride, and life from profit. Afraid to live and afraid to die, they do all they can to evade and shield their collapsed esteem, in order to justify their stagnation and secure their dependencies.

Most iterations of evil follow the same pattern, which is the opposite of what nature intends. The pattern of a fear-driven consciousness is:

1) *Panic* in response to existence,
2) Intellectual retraction or *evasion,*
3) Destructive Action, and
4) Penalty.

He runs *cognitively,* ingraining a behavioral pattern of constant disengagement and ends up only able and willing to see the world through the eyes and minds of those providing a tolerable means of escape. Have you ever tried to deal with someone who refused to accept the truth about something? Have you ever been threatened when you were too clear on a subject they couldn't face? Have you sensed the explosion that would come if you were straightforward? Have you ever proudly announced a true achievement, and watched others refuse to acknowledge that you even said anything? When their head isn't in the sand, they often see in body and spirit exactly what they want and move straight to our step four (reward), trying to take it from someone else. Evil has countless manifestations, all beginning as self-destructive cowardice, which then victimizes others in turn. Evading proper consciousness, the Fear-driven are free to ignore steps, to break the process up, and to replace steps with the effort of others, but the result is always the same: dysfunction, self-hatred, and their ever-expanding circle of destruction.

The function of the mind cannot be altered, as the function of the heart cannot. It has evolved into its most efficient design and can only be nourished by a proper diet, or starved and mangled by an improper diet. Evasion, repression, hysterics, emotional deadness, and the desire for any causeless reward are all a reflection of the misuse and malnourishment of the human mind. This is a neurological pattern—not the monopoly of any particular faith, but chosen one by one; a private, humiliating, heart-wrenching intellectual default. Reality is the last thing you want to have working against you!

Melding Cognition with Interaction

When alone, he faces an abyss—a void of identity—so he cannot be alone. He must exist within others, as with nature denied and consciousness negated, no other form of identity exists. Sentiment begins as *his view of himself* held by others, and becomes *his view of existence,* held by others. With life seen only second hand, *men* become the first axiom of his existence, and all of his primary standards become social.

For other Fear-driven, it was cemented years later, forced into submission by those holding a greater physical power. They were bullied, most often when looking up to adults for guidance and truth, and instead found themselves subjected to violence for a host of reasons: the awareness of what they weren't supposed to acknowledge, innocent questioning in the presence of denial—an early attempt to reason—all squashed by crude adults threatened by the honesty of a child.

On one side he sees a malevolent universe, which holds some dark, unknown peril at every sensation. On the other, he sees a menacing force much greater than his own, with no rationale to guide it. Reason clearly is not on the winning side. Stuck between the incapacity to face existence and men who disallow the process anyway—unable to deal with either—he gives in and uses his tools only enough to evade what he perceives as a danger.

As his *first* enemy is existence, his *second* becomes consciousness. Consciousness being the inescapable link to his first enemy and his only means to direct his elusion, he uses it to pull a barrier between himself and existence. The barrier can only be his *third* enemy—other men. He chooses to side with the least of these evils—the penalty he knows—subhuman brutality. He must face existence or Man to pursue his sustenance, and with existence an unknown road, the road of deceitful appeasement is provided by those demanding his submission. As he's motivated by fear and others attempt to motivate him *by* fear, his conclusion is inherently confirmed. *The Submission/Domination Axis* has in his mind, become inescapable and therefore *axiomatic.* The fundamental axioms of existence and consciousness have been replaced by the substitutes of men and their coercive relation to one another. Instead of independence, he looks forward to the day when *he* will be the dominant force and will no longer need to be afraid. Of course, he doesn't realize that his highest aspiration has been chosen by fear itself, whose tenets will henceforth rule his destiny.

The impact of this malady on human freedom should be clearer now: the Fear-driven response to an individual problem is a *social* answer. They *meld* the process of cognition with that of interaction—a fundamental relinquishment—something the Self-made would never do. They crouch behind the rocks during our step 3, hurling insults and stoning us for its attempt. Then they spring out at our step 4 to seize our reward.

Sociology should be the study of the most efficient means of human interaction. Instead, it is this melding—the interruption of independent judgment. For the Fear-driven, the process of interaction *cannot* lie beyond the process of cognition because for him, it is a key ingredient. *"We're all in this together"* is his motto, beginning with his own physical motion and control. Once born, we have no physical link to others; any collaboration is a secondary consideration. But social connections are his substitute for *causal* connections, which leads to the only style of human relationship he's willing to acknowledge: submission and domination.

The Submission/Domination Axis

"One hundred thousand lemmings can't be wrong."
-Graffito

Submission is the gauntlet through which all Fear-driven are borne. For the fledgling dominant, his first experience is submission to physical existence—an enemy offering no alternative, to whom he ascribes the power of a malevolent consciousness bent against him. His aspiration becomes to seize the dominant role and trounce on existence in turn (as sound thinking was first to go, next is civility). Violence and threats are only one side of the psychological coin however; the other side never got that far, and remains submissive.

Such sharks and shark bait need each other. The dominant needs someone to dominate. Fearing to face nature when no structured force exists for them to submit to, the submissive can't be alone either; it is a mutual dependency. One side fakes reality, takes no constructive action, and submits, feeling no potency. The other side fakes reality, takes no constructive action, and lashes out, drawing on a single potency—the power to destroy. Both are limited to the same physical capacity, but one exercises it, while the other will react only when cornered. Differing only by degrees of passive/ aggressive certainty, were they to reverse roles, the result would be the same. They're simply two impotent sides of the same intellectual default—the patsy and the killer, the squasher and the squashed, the dominant and the submissive.

The submissive is impotent in body, so his path to freedom and esteem is imagination. The dominant permits the unreality of the submissive, which honors and does not challenge his position. They team up, as in "Your schemes, my power." Abandoning reason is their tie. They believe there's no alternative to force and docility—that it is an *axiomatic* relationship. They cannot conceive of any other means, because they cannot conceive independently. Claiming faith as their substitute for thought, *wishing* and *force* comprise the two extremes along their scale of intellectual impotence. When reason is dropped, its void is always filled by variations of the Submission/Domination Axis.

Their relativism gives shape to mass movements and other forms of hysteria—lynch mobs, riots, and manias—all of mindless intentions and violent ends. In the Irrationally Dominant's mind, *stealing* is self-restitution. In the Submissive's mind, *alms* is self-restitution. The premise of mob-rule, the combination of stealing and alms in Altruist Communism—of all chained to all as an ideal—is its worst outgrowth.

The Irrationally Dominant

The Dominant can often deal with nature; it is the consciousness of others and his own in this regard, with which he cannot deal. Force substitutes as often as possible for any cognitive requirement. He likes to pick fights and be disrespectful as he tests for boundaries, pushing others to feel what he feels—the extreme tension of being one step away from explosion.

His identity and esteem come from the outside, so he must be sure that you know he's there. Most obvious in his teen years, he becomes a danger as he tries to get your attention. He has to assert his physical dominance not only to gain power over you, but to validate control over himself. He often confuses his own sense of feeling threatened with an attack, and he counter-attacks, where even telling you what to do is an imposition that justifies his abuse. In his most cowardly form, he waits for privacy to show you his darkest and truest attributes—providing a front to the rest. He won't share himself, as all he could reveal is panic. His life isn't what he wanted, having feared the responsibility of desire. Fundamentally unwilling to be productive, he equates earning a living with torture, so he's notoriously cheap. He abuses others—his wife, his children, his dog—to convince them they represent the level of worthless evil that he himself feels. He makes his family suffer a personal holocaust, which if put into words would say, *"I can't lead! I can't guide us to any values; I can't even lead myself. I don't know what it means to be a man; my only link to it is that I can hurt you."*

When nature removes his dominance through age, he retains the faculty of denial—none of it ever happened. How can he evade it? Simple; he's a coward. That is a pattern he has practiced all his life.

Strong people don't need obedience; they have nothing to gain from it. Chickens and quitters, no matter how well disguised, do. They must destroy us physically because they can't face us intellectually. Murder sometimes, is just one less person to convince.

Torture

From medieval times and before, the Dominant have shown their inventiveness with countless ways to dole out punishment and few if any, ways to celebrate human greatness. To torture another is to give voice to their own angst with sensory tools. Those who want to torture the senses are those tortured *by* them—nagged by the incessant flow of data, which they refuse to classify and use rationally. Their intention is to expand every source of pain. Maximum infliction is their goal, and their senses are heightened *only* to this end. For once they acknowledge the senses, and the only way they are willing to explore them, is in agony. It is a reenactment of how they feel—helpless and under the power of a malevolent force bent on their destruction.

In daily life, the Irrationally Dominant starts at home by making war against his family, keeping them fearful in order never to be challenged or questioned. Instead of fostering development of the young, he manipulates with confusion and fear. He kicks the dog and abuses the children, where molestation is just the sexual release of the same torment. To reassert his view of his own maturity, he seeks an adult confrontation by beating or harping on his spouse—another frail adversary. All he has to do to settle his conflicts is get mad, but conflicts are never settled this way, so he's *always* mad.

The Dominant tries to hide his ugliness, but it comes out anyway; it is never just domestic. His scale of abuse operates as high as his ambition permits—in his company, debasing his suppliers and associates, or in civics, enslaving provinces, states, or nations. He doesn't let you merge in traffic; to merge is to beat him. He has to prove to his ebbing and flowing audience that he's no patsy. Make a mistake and he rides you with his horn blaring. His productive effort amounts to the same: backstabbing, playing games, befriending, and then badmouthing. In the office, he makes a big deal out of your mistakes, amplifying the negative. Think about it: this is someone whose self-esteem is at risk in traffic, or just being looked at. How stable or fulfilled could he be in the important areas of his life? It is agitation he feels, and it is destruction he wants—to annoy, to pester and to irritate you in the way his fears and failures irritate him. If he has to win in traffic, it is a sure sign that he's losing in life.

At his least harmful, he simply bad-mouths and pesters. At his worst, he robs, tortures, and murders. He breaks into your home while you are sleeping. He stalks your wife and children. He mugs your parents. He keys your car. He can rob you in ways you've never dreamed of, but he has. To revel in torture is to confess the trauma of experiencing life as pain. The tantrum of never feeling good feelings is to amplify it. It is a crescendo, and a relief to be rid of. The Self-made crescendo is an explosion of joy—singing, dancing, and intimacy—in celebration of life. But fear-driven men consider virtue to be *carrying* the burden of pain—a concept they've saddled us with as well. And they wish us to ignore the warning as they do, to the same end. Misery loves company.

The Submissive

Witnessing the nature of the submissive first hand is downright medieval. We've all encountered the type. Eyes that say, *"I'll let reality be whatever you want if you protect me and promise to like me."* They will plead on their knees *not* to know that the standard of good is life and justice. This is what true pity is reserved for—the scared human animal, self-castrated, cowering before life.

Submissives automatically grant the role of dominance to others whether they wish to assume it or not. They play the card of weakness, believing those stronger must withstand any emotional torture as recompense for imposing their strength. The real conflict begins when their adversary isn't interested in dominance. Their role is lost. Civility is out of the question; it leads to reason, and their stamina falls far short of that. They are thinking, *"Why is he trying to convince me? Why doesn't he just take what he wants?"* The submissive considers reason to be weakness—a reflection of their own pleading, and will try to assume the dominant role. They shift from dodging a violence that isn't there, to imposing their own. As well, the dominant only sees reason as a greater power when it doesn't submit to his rants. He then attempts submission, destruction, or escape. To him, *to agree is to be out of control,* is to be submissive. Both swap sides in times of crisis, but they won't think.

Voluntary Enslavement

There is always a group of patsies for the killer and it is their job to deliver themselves, their children, and anyone else possible to their destruction. Many of those selling peace are only seeking your peaceful surrender to evil premises.

The dominant doesn't typically create or enact subversion; he just takes what he wants—you, me, any value. The submissive tries to get the same irrational benefits voluntarily. Violence is the province of the dominant, but the submissives have a wicked parallel: the subversion of morality. Instead of a tool to *aid* human progress, morality has been used as a weapon against mankind from the beginning of time. The Fear-driven can't afford to have you discover morality's true value; the responsibility it would impose on them is unthinkable. So instead, it has been used for torture. There is no more devastating a spiritual infliction than to be accused of being morally unfit; there is no more debilitating a threat than to be considered cognitively inadequate. There is no more embarrassing a demise, than physical destruction at the hands and limitations of an inferior mind.

Guilt is the spiritual fine for a known moral offense. When subverted, it is a submissive tool to make us feel bad about feeling good—a pure inversion. They have us believing that if anything is for ourselves, it is evil—it is against others. If our leaders tell us it is evil to sit down—something in life that we can't avoid doing—and we believe them, we will accept whatever punishment they hand down. Now, our energy is guided by atonement.

How did they get us to fall for it in the first place? Without a rational standard of good and evil, it was easy. Everyone has to enact sound principles if life is to continue, so all life actions are fair game to be labeled as evil but "necessary," such as sex, work, or personal ambition. Subjects of damnation are kept in flux, as inconsistent, unpredictable moral requirements assure dependency. If you wish to secure any further value, you have to join the gang. You will be harassed or risk being killed until you do. Sound familiar? If they stop you from advancing spiritually and making the correct moral connections, that is enough. We must be *independently* sure that our guilt is rationally earned, as it is a key tool of slavery. Add religion and it becomes a business. If they can alter your course in any way, they've earned significance in their eyes, and control is their primary intention.

Ridicule

Walking down a train platform in Lausanne, Switzerland in my twenties, I came upon two French-speaking girls. As I passed, our eyes met; I smiled and kept going. On the way back from viewing the schedules, I smiled again, but instead saw malicious eyes and a contemptuous voice trying in English, "You loser." I looked at her in humored astonishment that I was important enough a sight to openly degrade, and as she read my thoughts she lowered her head in shame...then I marveled at how far I had come. Two years earlier, such a thing would have been devastating; one year earlier, I would have been drawn into her hell long enough to give a hurtful or frightening reply, but now, my owned rhythm took precedence. I saw her essence and answered her as she had earned: identification and *dismissal.*

It is useful to identify the nature of what she did as being single so far, I've run across a number of times. She struck what she viewed as the worst possible blow one can deliver to the esteem of another; but what we define as good and bad, harmful or harmless, depends on our standard of value.

If we hold that our self-worth doesn't rely on the opinions of others, but relies solely on our capacity to sustain and enjoy life and our follow through, then no foundationless assertions can rattle us. The same is true when approaching someone you find attractive. They know only what you show them. If they say no, it means very little. Self-esteem only dies by suicide. Only its *pretense* can be killed by others.

People amped in the triumph of ridicule are the prime victims of such petty disturbances, discomforts and disapproval—a raw sensitivity to their own life's socially parasitic discontent. Insincerity is moral self-incrimination; it is a lie to oneself. I watch insincerity closely, because it is not a reflection of others, but of the futility of one's own stillborn aspirations. If you are looking down, you are no longer climbing. Still, we learn as children the power of ridicule. Beyond simple rottenness, it becomes excommunication or public stoning, a taste of power along the same line—feeding the sick curiosity of watching another living organism die, physically or spiritually.

Any mud thrown at an ideal is ultimately thrown at oneself. It becomes easier to bear, knowing that under their malice lies shattered dreams, hopeless longing, and an unreasoning fear that drives them to change their center of focus to you.

The Spirit Murderers

The Fear-driven's sabotage of rationality is kept private only so long. Soon, they have to transfer the vast negativity it generates. We hear that the good always prevails, but the truth is often, the best *don't* win. They get taken out by weapons not in their arsenal. If the only human danger were crude gunman, burglars, and other easily identified criminals, common law would be enough to safeguard civilization. The real danger is philosophical subversion: the false ideas behind human action in thought, relationships, art, and the social institutions designed for the supposed benefit of all.

No one could guess by whom and in how many ways their passion is drained, but one term describes the enemy: Spirit Murderers. Spirit Murderers come in many forms, all motivated by fear essentially, and hate ultimately, with one common social goal: to design and skin the perfect victim. They ride us, and hate us for our ability to carry them, so they try to rob us of our sense of living which holds adventure, endless possibility, and personal significance and replace it with the paranoia, insignificance, and helplessness that *they* chronically feel. So how do they do it? They disrupt *our* cognitive pattern. They turn our tools against us, by infusing us with the same detrimental patterns that led to their own spiritual suicide. If you want to untangle the bewildering motives of evil, just trace the proper pattern of cognition and watch where and how they default on it (In my 12 CD set, *Sovereignty*, I've done this for you. I delve deeply into the most common evils to offer a complete understanding of the Fear-driven mindset, and the psychology behind it).

The confusion they cause suppresses the true premise and intention of either side: that of life or death. This isn't accidental, of course. When an army is in front of a large gun, it will mix with the opposing side to nullify the weapon. This is what the Spirit Murderers have done with their default. If they can keep it from being seen, they can keep it from being annihilated. Their death patterns are interwoven throughout all living structures, and sickly enough, in our own moral confusion, we have woven ours around theirs as well. But with the moral pattern of cognition known, we can now choose sides openly.

A Fool's Paradise: The Birth of Altruism

Men are not born Spirit Murderers. It is an identity that fear-dominated minds assume, upon acquiring some sense of physical potency in the successful disregard of existence. He finds his home in a sub-structure that was prepared by other cowards over time; a societal structure requiring no mental effort—only obedience. In exchange for his servility, he gets protection from reality, which keeps him safely anonymous among the pack.

Disconnected from self-support, the main activity of his mind becomes his limitless imagination. As the better men abandon such quests for unreason early, those who remain *encourage it,* fostering his distance from reality. To his relief, the natural world *need not* be obeyed or even considered, as he can attain his desires through these others—handed to him without causation. This allows him to disavow the world he fears, and disassociated, he looks at the world without dread for the first time.

In his world everything is free; treats fall into his hands from the sky; the atmosphere is set for his pleasure, his subjects bow to him, and endless luxuries exist for his delight. He can claim that *by nature,* nothing is to be expected of him; that thought and its benefits should be automatic; that life should be provided to all as a minimum and require no effort. His guardians applaud his description of their heaven, and all his effort toward these values in real life, stops. He receives love and acceptance without relation to his actions, and the traits he sees in others that cannot be had without effort—strength, ability, bravery—his guardian's assure him are unimportant and without consequence—the products of luck. With all values being automatic, all of his guilt can be shed or reversed. He can now conclude that those engaging in effort are the ones lost in folly, and he can safely look down on them.

There is only one problem with this world—it isn't real. Ultimately, none of it works. It seems to at home, but in the real world, the active, courageous boy wins the race, saves the day, and gets the girl. The real world doesn't acknowledge his illusions. Here, there is no pride without achievement, there is no love without personal value and there is no life without effort. The girl he has a crush on doesn't know he exists; she has a crush on the boy whom his guardian's every statement has been designed to condemn. "Why would she want *him?*" he asks. Lied to and weakened by those closest, primarily himself, he isn't prepared to compete on wholesome grounds. He ends up thankful that the girl doesn't like him, intimidated by what her expectations would reveal.

From the beginning, his successful escape from responsibility achieved no esteem at all, but only left a void where esteem should have been. No matter what his inner world redefines truth as, authentic standards prevail in every endeavor: the smartest go the farthest, the best looking turn the most heads and the most confident and capable draw the most respect. Dulled by evasion, grimaced in anger and stifled by fear, his spiral has begun, where no happiness, pride or significance can be conjured—only bland safety. He knows he isn't *really* living. He can even acknowledge that those who help maintain his front are fakes, but he returns to them for the consolation the outer world withholds—solace for an irrational contempt.

How to Make a Monster

Looking out at those who did not fall to the same fear; those capable of experiencing the spiritual rewards of living—pride, confidence, love, and happiness, he witnesses the way his dream-girl looks at her knight. He recognizes the virtues the knight represents, and ultimately stares inward with the lost eyes of his greatest heartache. He sees that not having the traits of strength, bravery and ability, *do* hold consequences; consequences too terrible to contemplate. He admits, *"That is* what I could've been. All it would take is..." and fear overcomes him once again in response to the forbidden word—*independence*. He must look away, or he will realize what the good is *for*.

His choice is either to acknowledge the highest and pursue its image, or to destroy the vision and any evidence of it. It is the destruction of life he chooses. He shrinks from the challenge; he cannot accept that the responsibility for its creation is *his*. He can't risk failure and lost pride pursuing new values, when he must stand fast just to preserve the image of his faked values. But he sees life being lived by dynamic people, and cringes when he sees them win their dreams. "No!" he screams, in the face of truth. He can't make unreality real and he can't have what he wants, so he can't let it be possible for others.

He is not intent anymore on making the unworkable work, but on the deliberate destruction of what *does* work. He discovers he is not the only one dissatisfied with reality—the contempt is widespread. He finds a way has already been paved to transfer his burdens to honorable shoulders, through a collusive thought process developed against the productive by his fear-ridden predecessors. The battle has raged on for centuries, between independent men desiring civility and those impotent to pursue values, who require a blood sacrifice in every premise. His default has chosen his side, and he is taken under their wing. His youthful choices are rationalized by formal anti-concepts. He learns that his fear to venture into the world was only his binding love for his family; his submission to others was the ideal of selflessness, and his treason against life in misguiding children was a noble sacrifice for nurturing their esteem. Masking that they live *through* others, they claim instead to live *for* others.

They held their wounds up before the world to be healed, and through sympathy, brought *dependency* into moral focus. Declaring this the highest moral premise, they demand that all be chained to all, in an attempt to crush their prey by the very nature of their independence. In retaliation against existence and those able to deal with it, he learns to turn Man's productive tools against them, by infusing them with the same detrimental patterns that led to his own spiritual suicide.

He is not irredeemable, but as reform opposes his every conscious premise, we must interact from a point of safety. Developing that safety requires that we learn and accept what he has known all along. In other words, *know thine enemy.*

"It's what people know about themselves inside, that makes them afraid." —High Plains Drifter

There was a reason our Founding Fathers said "We hold these truths to be *self-evident.*" The ancient spiritual conflict has been a battle for control of Man's consciousness, and negation of mind is their primary tactic.

There are many parallels between what elicits the deepest feelings of horror in human beings, and the moral doctrines we have all been taught. Reading the Bible, you see the lure of unearned rewards, everlasting bliss, unlimited power over men and nature, and you get it all, just for believing. *"Join us, and your imagination reigns."* In an uncertain realm, they promise the certainty of no judgment, no effort, and nothing to worry about—but life doesn't work that way.

No man of esteem would want something for nothing. Freebies don't conjure that lecherous grasping reflex in us as it does in the Fear-driven. These are benefits only a parasite would long for—someone afraid of living—but this is the pursuit of most moralities today, and their default is *predictable.*

Fear is his target not to hit, but to avoid hitting—maneuvering to skim by unscathed. As he is always focused on fear, it is always near. The irrational wishes of a Fear-driven Man are at the root of every human evil at every level; slavery, Welfare, Nazism, white lies—all are ways around facing what one fears. Independent men need not make victims of others. The bloodiest regimes, the most savage crimes and the painful lives of lost dreams all began with a helpless slug at their core.

Death Premises

A death premise is defined in that it produces no values; it only consumes them. It has no replenishing factors, ending in the detriment or death of the consumer to follow, once the value is gone. The furtherance of a being by death pattern is parasitical by design, as it must seek conquest to sustain itself.

They have to prove to themselves and to the world that the actions they fear to perform are devoid of moral value. With that accomplished, they take the next step and declare them evil, which automatically declares the opposite of life-furthering action to be good. They clamp down wherever they can and dictate how things will be done, *or else*. But the nature of human progress doesn't recognize *"or else,"* and their aims are sometimes exposed for what they are actually seeking—a slave/master relationship.

Deception

To lie is to confess one's own living impotence—the personal conviction that life *can* be faked—that there *is* an alternate world that harbors bountiful treasures, much greater and much easier than the one that exists. Lies show one's *preference* for that world, a willing commitment to evade known facts in order to dance down the road of illusion, in pursuit of carrots which rationality forbids. The *get away with it* mentality sees *riches* as a result of dropping his mind. Lies are a form of wealth to him, a way to be a coward and have the hero's bounty as well.

Lying is proof of a cognitive dependency—one cannot lie to a rock or a tree, convince it that it is a loaf of bread or a house and then benefit from the lie. One can only deceive a consciousness in an attempt to secure some undeserved value—even from one's own. White lies are the blackest, as they are delivered under the guise of friendship. They act as a wedge, separating the victim from his expressed ideal.

All effort towards the proper value stops, as the victim is regarded as having reached it already. If he believes it, he is doomed to failure in attempting to display an attribute he doesn't have, competing with those who truly represent it. Believing he is in a different location on the road to his goal, with no chain of reason to tell him how he got there and no idea how to move forward, *he no longer moves,* and that is the end of values for him in that realm.

Lying just makes perception the enemy. When one attempts to live in defiance of truth, then truth becomes one's toxin. Lies mark our cognitive end in any realm, and where cognition stops, penalties start.

Self-made Man cannot lie or fake; reality is hard enough to keep straight. The hard-nosed image often criticized of the Self-made, is that he cannot be swayed with unreality. His stern intellect is not evil. It simply allows those who compromise, no moral escape.

Evasion of Self-Responsibility

Having spent his entire life, from early development into adulthood avoiding the whole concept of self, his first fundamental evasion is the realm of self-responsibility. Reflecting on his own actions, he considers the attributes of self to *originate outside of self,* alluding to every other conception as the source. With personal misgivings he wishes the external world would account for, the responsible parties are hand-picked according to expediency—God, destiny, other people, society, luck, genetics, past circumstances—all take their turn in the place of his guilt.

His mental effort is spent to hide the possibility of having any choice in the matter. He actually wishes that the barriers he invents *did* exist, to remove the mature obligation to act. The Self-made cannot fully conceive of or appreciate the power of his terror, and we are often left stunned when he plows through us to run the other way. Panic *replaces* his freedom to choose, and wipes out any desire for that freedom. It is no laughing matter; self-reliance is his greatest fear. He will kill or die to avoid the responsibility of independence.

Anti-Concept Formation

Words do not command reality, but only describe it. They cannot be tailored to an individual's wishes or weaknesses, and they do not alter existence. They are as rigid as scientific measurements, and the more precise we are in their use, the brighter are the benefits they make possible. But to a Spirit Murderer, words are a way of stealing: an attempt to loot the value of a concept's true meaning by stretching it to cover what it doesn't actually describe. In most circles, anti-concepts exist unchallenged, spreading and perpetuating without resistance, and to the trained ear, their death rattle can be heard in every sentence.

A concept is a mental integration of specific attributes. An *anti-concept* is a mental integration of *variable* attributes, subject to the interests of the wisher. It allows the user to hijack valuable concepts such as love, courage, and honor and install his own defining characteristics. A definition that lets any attribute comprise a thing, evicts it from the realm of identity, of measurement, and of focus. When *anything* defines a thing or a concept, *it no longer exists.* Anti-concept formation is the ultimate cognitive sin. It is not just the corruption of language, but of comprehension itself. In tribute to Aristotle, I call this *"A is Anything."*

Spirit Murderers intend to reverse or negate all attributes of Man and existence by any means possible. As we stair-step up, they head back down with whatever we have created. They have shadowed our progress through the evolution of thought: language. We use language to build; they use it to destroy. Consonant with the mislaid formation of their consciousness, so such a being uses language—not to clarify, but to form his Fear-driven outlook: obscure, uncertain, and out of control, without purpose or structure, to justify how he lives. His fuzzy, half-understood definitions can mean anything, or more to the point, nothing, and their insubstantiality leads him and anyone who listens as usual—to danger.

If they can mix and match cause and effect, they neurotically believe they can realize their imaginary world. Because a concept is not a material element like a rock or a tree, they think they can get away with subverting its identity. But such folly has never resulted in the values they try to cheat. This is the only time when they exclaim the great power of the human mind. Their method is simple. They see desirable products or traits in others and detach the benefits from the work expended to achieve them. Then, they reattach the benefits to whatever random actions they themselves have taken. They disconnect the guilt, shame, and poverty *they* suffer, and plug *that* in as the result of the producer's effort, in place of his rewards. It is easy—the producer works and gets no thanks for it and no reward, while the Spirit Murderer is free to remain irresponsible and incapable, gets treated like a king and enjoys the looted bounty. It may sound like a foolish child's game and is, but it has grown into the foundation of many religious, philosophical, and governmental systems around the world.

Still, it doesn't work; not on an individual level and not on a national level. A man can cannibalize, but cannot assume the stature of his victims. He can steal their property, but he cannot reproduce the bounty which he efforts only to take. The productive cannot be drained to serve the nonproductive without collapse of the system, on any scale that it is practiced. But the something for nothing mentality respects neither reason nor boundaries. Never having to face reality is too big a carrot to ignore, yet the reality is quite different. Most Spirit Murderers remain in a state of neurotic dysfunction—angry and helpless—functioning just enough to make it to work each day, grudgingly adhering to the minimum level of civility society requires. Their range is expanded politically though, by voting for those promising the sacred impossible.

Non-thought

Most Fear-driven use abstraction improperly, if ever. Even what they call "thinking" is suspect, as you cannot trust their means of differentiation. What anything means to them, is simply *what it means to others,* and they often only parrot what they hear. A viewpoint derived not from existence but from others does not qualify as thought, or as one's opinion. Thought is an independent process, revealing links back to the foundations of existence. His mental content was accepted without awareness of the roots leading back to its origin, and therefore he lacks the capacity to work with the knowledge itself.

Their shallow opinion however, is its own avenger—to damn with only a few facts has an alternate short-range equivalent—to *love* with only a few facts. They give their favor without firm identification and vent their dislike with the same willingness to approximate, and wonder why maintaining values and avoiding tragedies are so equally precarious. There is no escape from the penalties of a shoddy intellectual effort. With a fifty-piece puzzle in front of him, he tries to draw conclusions after he gets a few pieces. He wants everyone to pretend that the picture is complete, and that he is justified to move beyond it, and he does—straight into a void.

An anti-conceptual mentality will raise wages without expecting the product to cost more. He will cap consumer prices without regard for the price of energy. Ignoring the big picture questions his capacity to handle the living process of managing it, or to "run the chain," as I call it. But what begins as a lethargic byproduct of cowardice grows into the deliberate and irrational invalidation of sound reasoning, as well as the irrational *validation* of unsound reasoning. Then you are dealing with pros (inquisitors), and the game can get very dangerous indeed.

From a Spirit Murderer, you will hear nothing but approximations about facts and final verdicts about unknowable dementia. He fights to nullify the rational process of validation—the process he fears—in order to fix the impossibility of personal action, but his excuses remain dynamic, as do the accused sources of his own guilt. For a group whose slogan is "There are no absolutes," they hold as utterly absolute, the impossibility to pin any responsibility on themselves.

Spirit Murderers cannot afford admitting to an accurate definition of good and evil—they wish to allow no clean, rational view of innocence on one side or total contamination on the other. They see *"no need to go to extremes,"* in other words, no need for purity and no need to disinfect. Whenever I hear this, I think of the research laboratories or the dust and dirt free environment of the space shuttle pre-loading bay. I think of micrometers and other precision instruments measuring phenomena well beyond our sensory grasp. I think of the complex readouts on digital displays, where some miniscule variation can make a roomful of scientists cheer, or rise in astonishment. I think of my constant pursuit of pure, moral clarity and all it has given me. No need? Another word for *extreme* in this context is *true.* Extreme beauty, love, devotion to truth, accuracy, purity, physical awareness, knowledge, happiness, bounty, are all powerful forces that serve the living. Then again, living is not always one's intention. To avoid extremism in the context of identification, is to avoid exactness. They say, *"We are all just shades of grey,"* except for the best, and of course, the worst.

Enterprise of Mind

The strain of reality never gives the Fear-driven a moment's rest, so to him, peace is impossible. As his ideal is a mental state undisturbed by thought, his outward manifestations are simple extensions of this desire. To him, peace is a willing victim, and prosperity is a constant flow of unearned goods. But such gluttony is quickly identified—even by him—as a distraction, and his mind presses on for the true means of satisfying a natural craving—a productive (or destructive) endeavor.

Life allows no negation of purpose. A man's enterprise of mind—his fundamental purpose—*is* his expression of self-esteem, or his evasion of its lack. If a pointed plan is not chosen in life, random integration and disintegration *is* the resulting plan. When a Fear-driven Man is free not to consider life, *he doesn't.* He contemplates its opposite.

Spirit Murderers start with themselves. His enterprise is wholly in fraud, in a manic interest not to face his core default, and he spends a lifetime building a defense against it. His underlying theme in constant self-reflection is *"It isn't true."* His only belief in the power of the mind is in the success of his evasions. He says, *"If existence is whatever I want it to be, then what I did yesterday didn't happen. It is wiped off, even out of the minds of those who witnessed it. I can move ahead with a clean slate, ready for new filth."* What he doesn't realize in the folly is that most everything he enacts or supports, addresses his weaknesses directly.

Consumed with the protection and concealment of his flaws, he works hardest to validate his own futility. He reads the riot act on why goals aren't possible and why his destiny is not in his hands. Let him have the floor and you will hear how not even tomorrow can be planned, that discipline can't be expected of men, how they will squash any attempt at virtue, how morality is hopeless, how ability can't be learned, how no one can know anything, that men are evil cannibals by nature and the world is going to end any day now in chaos and calamity. What he is actually describing is *himself,* his hatred and fear for life and the fragile mental structure he has built. Stop him in his blind fury, and he might see that *he* is the one with human arms and legs dangling from his mouth.

Let him go on and you will hear of his illusory jackpot—the sales pitch that all values requiring effort to achieve in our world, require none in his. All of our earned pride and happiness is a preposterous illusion, and all of his illusions are a command. His heroics portray not the courage of action, but of inaction, not the beauty of strength, but of weakness, not the honor of rewarding intelligence, but of emanating pity. He need do nothing to meet these standards. Stepping farther, the practice of virtue—productivity—can be considered selfish treason in his world, and all treason, a virtuous sign of faith. As no mind is recognized, contradictions cannot be exposed. As there is no process of validation, no errors can be invalidated. His goal is to devise an environment where he can feel significant, without doing anything significant. He believes his *"get away with it"* mentality has created an alternate universe where he can be powerful too, without representing the virtues required. But the truth is *"his world"* isn't a world at all. To describe any part of it, he must give it form by damning reality as a point of departure. *It is the inverse of the world that exists*—nothing more. It is our world minus effort and responsibility—our world minus honesty, where a man lives not by acts of will, but by wishes. The joke is on his followers: eluding to a world where one's mind is replaced, only spurs the dilemma where one's mind becomes powerless.

Subjectivity

History is filled with stories of men overcoming great odds—obstacles often put there by other men—and accomplishing the unthinkable. They were fought every step of the way in the name of *avoiding* unsubstantiated disasters, while the achievers created railroads, factories, power grids, and the electric light. We hear how our acts of creation will bring destruction—a destruction that never comes. We are the Evil West: evil because our laws protect the rights of every man regardless of his *"connections,"* the connections that determine whether you live or die in those other countries. The best of the West work uphill against howling protests stirred within those intimidated by our endeavors, while our advances are enjoyed in silence. Everyone forgets the fight, but we don't. As a consequence, we as the Self-made are left more desolate, and with a strained respect for our fellow men in general.

What if there was a pattern to it? The main premise of a moral man is *life,* and he is proud of the volume of his tool chest—of the many ways he can bring it about. The main premise of an immoral man is *death,* and he derives significance by the many ways *he* can bring it about.

If you were to imagine the Fear-driven structure of mind, it is a constant, willed reversal of normal intellectual flow. Never intending any correction, it is fully dedicated to the completion of its reversal, believing it will arrive at the world *as it wishes it were.* Have you ever righted a rubber band just to see it twist itself back again? Inversion is his steady state, where he feels most comfortable, not because it is natural, but because he is so uncomfortable with the world as it is. *To back out* is his first premonition. Any step towards clarity is a step in the wrong direction, summoned by what is considered evil to the success of his fundamental goal. He prizes his evil as a reproach to life, works to preserve and foster it, and ultimately works to confirm his stubbornly irrational view of existence, by *empowering* it.

A key misdirection in the field of psychology is attempting to catalog every instance of such pathology. The Fear-driven combinations of default and senseless reasoning are *infinite,* multiplying as fast as it takes him to cower in response to any looming responsibility. All forms of psychopathology begin with the intentional or unintentional, self-assumed, dogmatic or cultural, misplacement of existence and consciousness in one's hierarchy of values—placing consciousness first, *before* what it is conscious *of*—to believe consciousness to be a power determining existence itself, versus its true role of observation. This is the choice and difference between *objectivity* and *subjectivity.*

Psychology is *not* the study of human thought and action—*philosophy* is. That semiconscious behavioral elements make up the vast majority of human action and relegate themselves to psychoanalysis is due to the present moral limitations on cognitive advancement—*not* due to a fault in the nature of the species.

Metaphor and Reality Swapping

We know that workers exist in their jobs voluntarily, and can quit whenever they want. We know that employers offer a position and a salary to those qualified, and we can accept it or say no—neither can resort to force. American free enterprise is not a slave/master relationship, but metaphorically in the press, it has always been treated as one. Voluntary involvement in American business has never been cutthroat competition; that is a mob term. Without the writer's poetic chains, there is no justification for his animosity. Either his readers can't tell the difference between metaphor and reality, or the *"get away with it"* mentality simply appreciates the lines being blurred in their favor, anticipating an undeserved windfall if they act as an injured party. Their intention is not to achieve equal opportunity for the less endowed—they already have that—but to return to the violence of the dark ages and emerge above our greatest men as their master.

Metaphor and reality swapping is driven by the desire to be rewarded for irrationality. The Fear-driven think *"Wouldn't it be nice if I could spill some coffee and retire,"* and as juror, they allow someone else to do just that. Their generic question in all contexts is, *"Wouldn't it be nice if we could wish instead of think?"* and every attempt to make it possible just dims humanity with infection. It manifests itself as business-killing union demands, outrageous awards in parasitical lawsuits, insurance scams and welfare—all justified through a melodramatic loss, impossible to validate or measure. The winnings then foster lower class concerns, whose existence relies solely on the spread of the infection, robbing mankind of a brighter future.

False Equality

Our Constitution says that *"all men are created equal,"* but Spirit Murderers extrapolate this *past* a man's creation, to claim it is a lifelong chain on all men obligating them never to outpace each other, and if so, requiring an equal distribution of their wealth to compensate for all human attributes which are clearly *not* equal—honesty, effort, willingness, et cetera.

Our most significant traits are chosen by us. We all have hopes and dreams, but we vary greatly in our ambition for their pursuit, which produces the Self-made bounty a Spirit Murderer sees as worth looting. Recalling Forrest Gump who becomes a millionaire even with numerous—including mental—handicaps, would the fighters for supposed equality *desire* to be retarded? No, it is his money and honor they are eager to divide. Take away subversive language, and it comes down to the simple abrogation of values created by those willing, in favor of those who aren't.

The perfect contrast is that the Self-made all strive to be *unique,* while the Fear-driven want to blend in and hide. From the faceless masses, they demand that all men be provided with a prosperous life as a minimum on which to build, unwilling to start where nature starts us all. Who is to provide it? This kind of equality just leads to another slave/master form of cannibalism, as confiscation is their only means to achieve it. Equality is a legal concept only, meaning no man is born with special privileges denied to others. It doesn't pursue happiness *for* them, or grant them any products produced by others, but only clears their path of the unjust obstacles witnessed throughout history.

That those of greater ability, effort, and tenacity should live under threat of confiscation by those less endowed or less willing, is an abomination. That the smooth functioning ideas of a thoughtful, civil discipline should be subordinated to the unworkable tantrums of those demanding equality *as measured in asset value alone,* but never in effort, is deplorable. Moral? Like hell it is.

Materialism and Profit

Life's lovers intend to earn and therefore *deserve* the best the world has to offer. Materialism is an anti-concept which damns this desire as a spiritually bankrupt, destructive pursuit. In the most rudimentary separation, it considers the body and mind to be two halves of a man that are fiercely at odds—the modern equivalent of religion's *"man fighting for his soul."* They claim they can put him back on track, exclaiming that spirituality can only be achieved by renouncing all material interests and necessities. The anti-concept is further narrowed as no intellectual pursuit is considered spiritual, omitting whatever could offend the non-thinking, non-producing man. In true Fear-driven fashion, they look down on the physical world where they have no power, and look up to the spiritual where they have no responsibility.

In their world, spiritual pursuits must yield no hard-earned clarity or material advantages, just some empty, unquestionable, eternal bliss. Why is *that* spiritual; because it is the Hindu's answer? Centuries of monks have passed through time, sitting Indian-style in silence with steepled hands and have brought to the world a value amounting to exactly…nothing. Their credo is *mindlessness* as the price of spirituality and *stagnation* as the price of peace—not a healthy pattern to follow. Why renounce the material world? *"Man's greed"* would be their response, and the only way around wanting something improperly—as the

Fear-driven see no alternative—is to want nothing. The only way for them not to harm is not to move. But greed or any desire, great or small, is only wrong when one seeks the unearned.

Beginning with the obvious, a human being is an entity of matter *and* consciousness, requiring material *and* spiritual products to sustain itself. Should we damn our bodies because they are never done consuming food? Every day, on and on, nourish, expel, nourish, expel—and Man's spirit runs the same cycle. Spirit Murderers deny nature's cycle and decide they are done learning—what I call the *Finished Product*. Their intellectual growth stalls, cutting off their spirit as well. Happy people do not seek or settle for an intellectually or physically static state of being, at any age. There is no such thing as a mindless body or a bodiless mind, and a man cannot live lacking either. To survive, he must continue to feed both. They describe their wonderful out-of-body experiences, but what do you think their body is doing while they are off floating in no-man's land? Keeping them alive is all.

Breathe easily when a man is after money and luxuries he is willing to *earn,* because when he isn't, he is after control. The Spirit Murderers are responsible for wanting the unearned in *both* realms; the concept of materialism was created by them, in self-restraint supposedly solved by them, and the Finished Product was its result. This cold, mindless, dead relation to matter and spirit has nothing to do with us, so we should leave them to it.

Self-made Man *can and does* act without harming. Most forget that those accused of being materialist, often put many unpaid years into their fields before any profit is realized, if at all. And profit, damned for centuries, is a basic necessity of life, the requirement that one stays ahead of even—in body and spirit. It is the third step of cognition, the act of creation—that brings the human spirit to life. It is the fourth step of cognition—validation, whose equivalent in work is profit, which determines whether we are on course. Whether our interest is commercial, romantic or both, it is *not* evil or wasteful as the Spirit Murderers claim, but *essential:* the very fiber of our self-esteem, and the key to the deepest spirituality a man can ever hope to reach—and they know it.

To know that our divine inspiration has a productive purpose—that it brings joy to others and prosperity to ourselves, that our energy serves a sum, not to be lost in the past, but a value to be brought forward with every day of our lives—develops a moral inertia that supercharges our exhilaration for living, bringing to fruition a height of personal significance almost too precious to contemplate.

False Proverbs

After a while, cultural trends form to reveal the Fear-driven's favorite approaches to impotence. Here are a number of common sayings rooted in cowardice that have been an endless source of moral irritation for Man:

"There are no absolutes in life" or "Nothing is certain" versus our vast awareness of unchanging natural standards discovered with every step up the ladder of science. You don't have to speak to a nuclear physicist to verify whether or not there *are* absolutes; ask anyone with a checking account. The next time you hear this, ask the speaker to go step on a rake a few times to see if he notices a trend.

"Judge not, lest ye be judged" versus the coherent identification of a man's adherence to life-furthering principles, *as well as one's own.* Negating the value of judgment implies that thought itself is an act of evil. If they declare the brain to be useless, then why respect the content of theirs? Jesus meant that men should not judge each other *falsely,* by irrational standards—nothing more.

When someone says they **"didn't have the heart"** to do or say something—it means they are being heartless, and it is true. Gutless too. We don't have to kick someone when they are down, but when they are *asking* for help, a tactful discipline is called into action. Offering frank advice communicates your belief in their capacity to reach the stature they seek, which directly attributes to yours.

"In this day and age", "At this time," and "In this environment," are valid only for strategy; not to justify compromising with or submitting to corruption.

"That's old-fashioned", "That's out of date," or "You have to change with the times." Likewise, the untried and new is also not to be trusted. This may be suitable to clothing fashions, but they want to apply it to physics as a universal axiom.

A premise dealing with organic life identified 2500 years ago isn't any less valid than a discovery of five minutes ago. Sir Isaac Newton's Laws of Motion still apply, as do what led to their discovery—Aristotle's Laws of Logic. Axioms are good for *all* time, regardless of when they are discovered; and concerns such as luxury and fashion remain possible only as long as men respect them. Likewise, Fear-driven premises were wrong 2000 years ago, are still wrong, and always will be.

"If you want it *bad* enough." Negatively enough, or just intensely enough? A strong desire is *not* evil; that is precisely why it is labeled as bad.

"You have to give something back." Originally a mob custom, this false premise intends to stain life-furthering productivity, implying that commerce is a form of robbery.

"Not everyone can be wealthy." Everyone can be as wealthy as the effort they are willing to expend. We are all responsible for our immediate environment; whether we empty the garbage or let it rot, whether we live in a pigsty or not is up to us. Money is the mass-acknowledged measure of wealth, but the forms of wealth are infinite. The feeling of wealth is different for every one of us. A fisherman may desire the latest vessel and the ability to yield the greatest bounty. Another may imagine a fleet of exotic cars and the capacity to drive them expertly, right to their limits. Another may desire a beautiful landscape, a clean canvas and the time and skill to fill it. Men have infinitely different dreams, yet all share the same format, revolving around money, time, and skill. As long as *we* remain the source of our dynamic wealth—not a rich spouse or parent—the door to our deepest self-esteem remains open.

"There is good in the lowest." The Fear-driven always look for value in remote places, ignoring wherever value is obvious. Mining for that minute percentage is only a diversion to guard what they consider the overwhelming sum of their being—incompetence and evil.

"He or she has potential." *Everyone* has potential. What you should be looking for is *kinetic*. Objects in motion tend to stay in motion, just as still objects tend to stay still. If one's predisposition is to do nothing, you have an uphill battle on your hands. Forced into action, the Fear-driven look to dig and dive right back into another foxhole. Don't kid yourself; they seek safety—not rewards. They have to get out of *that* hole alone.

"Happiness is fleeting." Accepting no clear definition for happiness wipes out their obligation to uphold the standards that would lure it into their lives *as a constant*—just like love.

"A person is a product of his environment." Our lives and character are molded by many causative factors, but we are responsible for managing *all* of them. Their effect on us is our *objective* pride or our *subjective* guilt.

"Grow up!" They mean that to grow up is to give up. To stand by convictions is to be cold and cruel. To tell lies is merciful; to be honest is rude. They call passion comical, and comedy becomes cynical. Twisting these definitions fakes to themselves that what they gave up wasn't worth reaching anyway.

We all decide what is sufficient to stop us. It is rare to encounter someone who doesn't stoop to the dishonesty of declaring values no longer to *be* values, once they have given up their pursuit.

"Loosen Up!" They want us to loosen up, but notice that we have few, if any, manic tendencies. What they actually mean, is that as one lets one's hair down, we should learn to let our premises down—to loosen our grasp on consciousness—yet *their* grasp is the reason for their mania. Self-made Men are masters of living, so reality is never the subject of their escape. We can spin our wheels, work hard, be light, be serious, do anything, buy anything, and go anywhere, all driven by our deepest passions in life—now *that* is freedom. Without a firm grasp on reality and purpose, one cannot and shouldn't be able to, relax.

Here are a few more:

"Patience is a virtue" versus pushing past barriers to accomplish one's objective. *"Money is the root of all evil"* versus acknowledging the mature civility of voluntary exchange between men. *"Speed kills"* versus the actual culprit, irresponsibility. *"Man is a creature of circumstance"* versus self-responsibility. *"It takes money to make money"* versus creativity. *"God-given talents"* versus acknowledging effort. *"Luck"* versus the earned and deserved. *"Unlucky"* versus lazy and afraid. *"No man is an island"* versus independence. *"Better to play it safe"* versus a fully conscious, pioneering attitude. *"We are just insignificant specks of dust floating through time"* versus proper contextual significance. *"No one can prove anything"* versus a rational progression of thought.

Such statements are driven by the secret desire to see their victims fail as they did. Such falsehoods are countless; these are only what have most often irritated me. Let your own understanding of life-furthering standards uncover and weed out the rest.

Chapter Five

The Core Mental Weapons of Our Slave-Masters

"Yours was the code of life...What, then, is theirs?"
—Atlas Shrugged

The two types of men—the Self-made and the Fear-driven—tend to act consonant with their inner motivation in all things. In time, we will come to understand them and how their actions are extrapolated into all the realms of Man, but for now, I want to expose their most critical violations—the building blocks they use in all higher anti-concepts—by which they have wrought devastation throughout the world, and you might be surprised at how common they are.

There was a reason our Founding Fathers said "We hold these truths to be *self-evident*." The ancient spiritual conflict has been a battle for control of Man's consciousness, and the negation of mind is their primary tactic. The Spirit Murderers have undercut the Self-made every step of the way, to keep the genie of intellectual sovereignty in a bottle. To gain control of a man, one must destroy his intellectual independence. To this end for millennia, the parasites have subverted every living premise, dividing cause from result, work from reward, and pride from choice. Only the unproductive, the fear-ridden and the incompetent could psychologically benefit from keeping the productive, the self-confident and the able in a state of moral uncertainty. So like any scheming dictator, they began stripping us of our defenses when we were just children. They took the radiant, shining standards of our love and made it unconditional. Original Sin and its modern descendent, environmentalism, damned the very nature of Man and robbed us of our innocence. They made off with the stability our virtue created and left us to answer their disasters. They took our gifts and made them sacrifices. They took our idols and replaced them with infirmities. They labeled us grafters if we worked hard, taking our honor and our pride. They attacked the living purpose of every man by claiming that any self-motivated action was sadistic; while the pursuit of money was considered pure hedonistic greed. Now this is important: By denying us individual purpose, we became a society that could work for *nothing but money.* Their trap was complete and the circle closed.

Impotence of Mind

To discredit thought, Spirit Murderers rely on claims that the mind acts as a tool of distortion, not of precision. They frame our intellectual development throughout history as exploded fallacies instead of a positive view for what actually happens: greater precision, for lives lived better and longer. As our knowledge and techniques advance, we reintegrate our data to provide more efficient and often revolutionary solutions, but this essential element of cognition is most often used as an example of the futility of all knowledge.

They begin in ways you wouldn't suspect, gently undercutting with such questions as, *"What came first? The chicken or the egg?"* and because we falter in response to the unexpected, they claim the mind *by its nature* is unreliable. Wait a minute while I answer them: "Okay idiot, the chicken. Between the two it is the only one capable of sustaining itself in nature. The existence of a living entity precedes its *attributes*—among which includes its reproductive process." Their intention becomes clear with what follows: other questions bearing no consequence in our lives such as, "So where do *we* come from?" "The scientific method has been disproved long ago" they say, because some obscure estimate about the universe was in experience found to be inaccurate (disregarding the incredible advances required to establish that fact). "That proves" they claim with glee, "that thinking is futile," and (forgetting that they are men too), "that mankind is a joke; everything he has ever done has been proved wrong. He can't get anything right; so why does he think he is so great?" Let me get this straight: We were wrong about gravity and it goes the other way now? Food kills us and poison is actually healthy? Civilization no longer requires gas, electricity, or running water? Earth no longer spins in a day? We don't actually breathe air? No, they just want us to believe that our "illusion of control" can be shaken by any senseless proposition they forward.

They rejoice in temporary relief when we fall short, needing to believe that to try is as futile as doing nothing. They long to see their own worst view of themselves confirmed as a condition of *all men,* eager to paint the productive as clowns to be laughed at. Every show I have ever seen on invention starts off with that bouncing helicopter and the goofy whistle noises. Could you imagine if Thomas Edison had to face a room full of such people snickering and hollering at every one of his ten thousand attempts? You'd be sitting in the dark right now.

Building a monument to Man is a delicate and heroic effort, be it a symphony, an enterprise, or the United States of America. The Spirit Murderers have always had it easier because no matter what heights we reach, it is all downhill for them.

Emergency Ethics

A favorite story of mine has a young man skipping clams that had washed ashore, back into the ocean. Another man approaches him and looking down the coast, exclaims, *"Why bother? You can't save them all; it doesn't matter anyway."* Reaching for another, he replies, *"It matters to this one."* Now, this can be interpreted in two ways by either mindset. That it is our duty to spend our lives helping every slug that falls short of life's requirements, or as a profound respect for *every* life—for life *as such*—to be prized first and foremost, by the one who is living it.

It may be true in situations of emergency that food and shelter must be had or life cannot continue, but to the fear-ridden, *everything* is an emergency. They make *their* default *our* priority at every turn, saying, "What are *we* going to do? We need food and we need it now; there is no time to investigate the cause of our plight. It exists for whatever reason, and it must be quelled or we will die. Oh, and four hours from now, it will happen again." A ship sinking, a house burning down, an earthquake, or a car-accident *are* tragic events requiring immediate attention to restore the normal flow of life. But the penalties of incompetence, general poverty, denial, cowardice, and lethargy—basic challenges in life with which we *all* must deal, are *not* among them.

We have all encountered emergency ethics in their view of love: *"If I were drowning, would you give your life to save me?"* Their focus is not on values to be shared, but on values to be destroyed. We hear 'disaster scenarios to prove our moral worth' everywhere, implying that emergencies are the standard by which to gauge all moral action. But is this standard justified? No. In the United States alone, 4% of yearly *deaths* are attributed to accidents, amounting to 0.0003% of the U.S. population lost—*less* than those lost to the flu. With figures such as these, there are no grounds to consider mankind as precariously clinging to life, nor to justify using emergency situations to define our moral code.

Sacrifice

When the rational mind is negated as our means of survival, conquest becomes the only alternative. Notice how sacrifice gives no pattern for creation or production—only for expropriation and consumption. It is a death pattern. If a process cannot sustain one man alone, but instead uses him up, not considering his life as the goal but as expendable fuel for *another* purpose, then it is wrong by design—it is evil. Its continuation is found only in new victims.

In ethics, sacrifice is an instrument of those who simply intend to leave you with less. *Sacrifice* is the destruction of values—death by slow or fast torture—nothing else. It is *not* a moral concept, but one of the most corruptly milked anti-life concepts of the Spirit Murderers. It is not about what is moral; it is about the destruction of those who are. If you agree to spill your blood for a cause, what will follow is not divine serenity, but demands for more.

Sacrifice is easy for Spirit Murderers to propound; they have nothing to sacrifice. Self-sacrifice is an indication—not of Mother Teresa goodness, but of incompetence. It is sold as a beautiful tribute to others, but its practical function is to replace one defaulted life with another. Each of us is a physiological whole. There is no way to part ourselves out and survive too. The call for sacrifice is the surest sign that a leader needs to step down.

Sound morality is not defined by borderline cases, miniscule percentages, or poetic delusions and neither is sound law. Sacrifice in civil times is clearly well outside its proper borders. It may tragically occur in the rarest of situations, but over 99.9% of the time, we live by *another* standard, which is the exact opposite of sacrifice. What defines true morality—just as in nature, just as in breathing—is the peaceful accumulation of physical and spiritual nutrients for the preservation and advancement of life—primarily our own; just what most of us do every day.

Selflessness

Every human being is a sum of virtues. If you become a greater sum, the world is richer for it. Selflessness demands the opposite: that you skin yourself alive giving everything to others, gauging your moral worth to how thoroughly you can rake over the most sensitive areas of your body and mind, without reaction. By their code, if you are self-abasing enough to catapult yourself into stagnant filth, you win, but not if you are still breathing. They imply that the only alternative to selflessness is to run others over—to be *selfish*—leaving no room for and never mentioning ...civility—a rational coexistence between men.

Claiming the best self must be selfless is as stupid as claiming the best airplane must be *plane*less. It is another term meant only to cause moral hesitation. The Self-made know better, and treat any mention of *selfless* expectations or *selfish* denunciations as an alarm for the acute awareness of motive. There is no selfless giving, without a self that *does* the giving. *Nothing human is selfless. Selves* do the work of life. Since they fear the self and don't use theirs, they need yours. Sooner or later, we had to come to the truth of the matter: haters of the self-sustaining, hate *themselves.*

Unconditional Love

When you pick out a Christmas tree, do you just grab the one closest to the car, or do you apply a set of standards? Unconditional love is the mother of all anti-concepts, the spiritual pinnacle of the irresponsible and un-worked for, eliminating the Fear-driven's two chief enemies: thought and effort. On the part of the grantor, it is the escape of determining standards; on the part of the grantee, it is the escape of upholding them.

Before I understood the issue, I would fantasize about what kind of woman I could make a lifelong commitment to—the one I could love *"unconditionally"*: the smell of her hair, the beautiful smile, the lovely figure, and a depth of sincerity and passionate ambition to match my own. Eventually I realized that in order for me to love her unconditionally, she would have to meet such rigid standards that her predefined virtue became Condition City! I was told my view of it was all wrong; I had mistaken it for complete confidence in another person (silly me). The purpose of unconditional love was *not* to project ideals and dream of an enchanted future to grow to be worthy of, but the unfiltered adoration of whatever drifts along at any time. How inspiring!

Then I saw the fundamental intent of unconditional love—to suspend consciousness: *the key element disallowed in the concept.* Love, a product of evaluation, was to be given without using *the tool* of evaluation—the mind.

Remember, unconditional love is *without* condition; selfless love is *without* cognitive appraisal; free love is *without* spiritual compensation. All are something for nothing, which in the physical realm is called theft. Spirit Murderers cannot accept that love is a reward for merit. Notice the hypocrisy: They claimed we must love everything, but we found virtues quickly excluded—didn't we—as they grimace at any true achievement. They made us feel guilty for our fulfillment in the presence of their pain—*guilty for practicing the moral patterns of life* and for gaining their proper result—pride. They successfully transmitted the bitterness which dwells in their own hearts—the second key to their *true* plan—*no reward for anyone.* Our only real guilt is that we fell for it.

The truth about unconditional love is that it shares the same source as race hate: a non-objectively-founded, non-cognitive appraisal. Why sidestep appraisal? For the same reason they wish to dodge the cash register in a store: to get away with life without practicing the virtues required by life. Uncovering its true intent, unconditional love is a reproach, in hatred for all human values; the values it was created to defy. It allows them on a spiritual level, just what they desire on the physical—to get away with murder. Conceptually its true meaning is *mindless approval*—a contradiction in terms. Approval presupposes a mind that approves. Love, presupposes a *self* that does the loving. As they deny Man his perceptions and perceptions are sensory-based, by their own definition, *it is senseless.* If your love can be had for nothing, then that is simply a declaration of its value, which *is* nothing, and of the corrupt moral premises which gave it that value.

True love is not the all-accepting, all-forgiving garbage can they claim it to be; it is just the opposite. Love is a precious reward—*a positive response to admirable traits*—and every human being, from the most innocent child to the most wicked, seething Spirit Murderer, knows it.

Infirmity Worship

The last moral atrocity I will speak of is infirmity worship. Take a look at what is universally considered the domain of moral action: doling out soup to the poor, emptying bed-pans with a smile, and being proudly victimized by the wretched: hand-outs, volunteer work, and martyrdom. They uphold as our ideal—as our reason for living and as proof of our goodness—servitude to the most indigent, inattentive, and unstable people. In our quest for nobility, we inherently seek a shrine: a hero's pedestal. They present to us instead, a hospital ward of living nightmares to attend to, which offend and retract every sense—without mind, without joy, and without hope. It is particularly painful as we are wide open in that moment, anticipating a deserved elation, and their timing is no coincidence. The pride we wish to express comes from our life-sustaining productivity; a sum that grows every day; a source they refuse to acknowledge.

They hand to us as the climax of our productive effort not honors, but a stupid grin under a chef's hat, *"giving something back"* at the local soup kitchen, implying that our normal occupation is a form of robbery. Our most significant moral progress has been prompted and maintained by science and industry, and has gone completely unnoticed as such, even by us, as we have been taught to believe that moral action means the *distribution* of goods and services required to sustain anonymous, immediate needs, without any consideration for their source. God we've been fools. The business of mankind—the production and exchange of products—is *not* evil; it keeps us all alive! It is the *means* of *civil* human living. We have fought for centuries to justify the existence of our business world, lacking the one weapon that would assure victory; the knowledge that it is *moral.*

And have you ever *tried* turning the other cheek to a criminal? So how was the hospital food? They tell us to permit and forgive any evil, therefore placing the whole burden of responsible action upon the innocent. If you agree with them, watch out! They will probably try to mug you on the way home. Does it make sense that our moral worthiness is tied to whether or not we can catch a speeding bullet and reform the shooter in the process? Do they offer a moral code for the time when we are *not* starving to death or dangling from cliffs? Does the productive ninety-eight percent need focus on the ailing two percent and fall victim to the criminal .01% in order to be virtuous? With a ratio of more than fifty-to-one, you can't possibly spend your life serving those in need. Does that mean that you spend the other ninety-eight percent of life doing things that are immoral? In their code, that is exactly what they mean, and culturally it is considered a foregone conclusion.

The results should be clear now: If the mind is negated, men's actions will be *mindless*. If men preach selflessness, *selves* will be destroyed. If they preach unconditional love, the conditions will be deplorable. The Spirit Murderers ask us to worship the sick, as a semiconscious acknowledgment of *their own* condition. Their psychological motive is the exact inverse of the Self-made. We worship the strong, the able, and the competent, because we actively seek to expand our own strength, ability, and competence. *We* respect living values and practice living patterns to attain them. *They* claim to respect living values, but practice *death* patterns to attain them. Health, wealth, and prosperity are touted on both sides, but while one side initiates the precursors to make them happen, the other does not; then, of course, they are just as surprised when their ends match their means and they achieve destruction instead. We may try to excuse them by claiming *"they know not what they do,"* but one must identify a thing's nature to except or reject it. To scream *"No!"* is to *understand.* All men have dreams, but only Self-made Man exalts the *effort* necessary to achieve them. Spirit Murderers skip the middle steps of cognition in all of these anti-concepts, and move straight to reward. They *See* and they *Seize,* two-stepping their way to destruction, twisting morality against life just to pacify their own madness.

Proper moral standards permit no breach with rationality. Self-made Man doesn't practice unconditional love; his condition is *life,* and all the discipline necessary to see its implications: eyes that see beautiful actions, ears that hear beautiful premises, and a mind that can tell the difference.

Sound civilization stair-steps up from sound coherence, to sound individual, to productive groups of mature individuals. Still, self-hatred drives the Spirit Murderer to wipe out the individual. To cover their cowardice, they pretend that any action of *the self* is vulgar, improper, destructive, and at the extreme of their own capacity to deceive themselves, to be insane. Just like *Invasion of the Body Snatchers,* they scream when they recognize a being who is still connected with the world of personal wants and desires—of passionate ambition and meaning—rousing the others to swarm and devour him. It is as if their view of morality came straight out of a Stephen King novel!

Everyone dreads the horrible feeling of a moral failure—no one wants to be that kind of outsider. Guilt is a correctional facility in itself for those who really *want* to live; but it is a brutal trauma to experience if undeserved, and is a sacrilege if imposed dishonestly. When you work hard and accomplish something great, then hear you are a greedy, selfish hater of those less endowed, you *should* be mad. When we reach our limit of tolerance and become offended, they'll tell us not to take it personally. I'm here to tell you, take it personally. Look at your accuser. Steady eyes will see the way.

Victim to Murderer: The Compromiser

"You never got out, you simply added yourself to the things they ran." —The Fountainhead

The most tragic social error of a producer is that through his foolish generosity, he often creates the illusion that a value can be had for a much lower price than reality sets. Perhaps as reality won't bend, he feels he has to, and rushes to catch their falling self-image. He creates the illusion that half-truths and half-lies can save a person, but then, half-truths and half-lies can damn a person. He spends his life faking the esteem of the first, while dodging the bullets of the second. He never questions their motive.

Unable to let them down in a drastic mix of cognition and interaction, the compromiser becomes responsible for the emotional stability of others. They harp on him, wearing him down with pressure and negativity, hen-pecking him to where he doubts his own judgment, bringing his very perception into question. Tortured *by them* for his clarity and weakened *by nature* for incoherence, he soon doubts his own sanity. With so few to support his logic and so many against, he gives in and follows the peckers through the process of identification. They push as far into his cognition as he allows, mixing his heroic effort with their dissatisfaction, masked as the moral failure of *his* interaction—a cognitive criticism impossible to ignore. He takes responsibility for all productive actions and exchanges the rewards for a hostile peace. His great skill is used to achieve aims no productive person would pursue and which the shallow can't reach alone. He is left as miserable as if he never used his mind in the first place.

Warrior Note: *Mixing cognition with interaction paves the way to spiritual suicide.*

There is another name Spirit Murderers give to those who valiantly subordinate themselves to others: pushover. His proper action would be to show the pattern to fulfillment for them to follow, but that is not what they want. It provokes the sneering look normally reserved for insects: *"Don't try to impose your filthy evil on me."* They want *his* life-generating power on *their* terms.

A compromiser believes in rational ideals, but permits the notion that rational discipline is not the only way to achieve them. He looks for an irrational middle ground—a balance between good and evil resulting in an anorexic, guilt-ridden good and a plump, blood-sustained evil. A balance between good and evil implies they *both* get what they want. But as the good has nothing to gain from evil, the premises of independence and life-production end up bent to serve dependence and life-destruction.

The most difficult battles in life will be with the Compromisers. He will reproach his peers, saying "I'm strong enough to carry them. I can handle it; you are the one who can't." *Sure* he can; it only took his joy and stripped the very meaning out of his life. It is their fault the Spirit Murderers reach as high as they do; their evasion opened the door and permitted their poison to infiltrate every realm. The Fear-driven have no power alone, but with *their* premises guiding *his* creative action, they built the atom bomb. If he stepped aside, he would cringe to see what their true incompatibility has been all along. Left to their own devices, they would have no choice but to get real, find other prey or become plain criminals. People who make you live under threats, pressure, and constant disapproval don't love you. They don't love anything. Until compromisers understand that a life-respecting system *does not* require victims, we have to insulate ourselves from their Fear-driven psychological limitations.

Warrior Note: *Our resistance to them must reflect their resistance to virtue.*

Familial demands, charitable foundations, money grants—this is how the fledgling Self-made get tangled and earn shame for their effort instead of the reward of solemnity and a moral-intellectual scope and power beyond anything their charity could achieve. It is treason not to defend life and all that leads to it.

Like a mouse kicking an elephant, Spirit Murderers must get us to accept that we are powerless. So they do their dance, knowing there is a great danger in our implicit premises. Realizing what that danger is, is to discover that the power is ours.

Self-Made Man versus the Spirit Murderer

Now let's get to the *real* issue. Why can't we as the Self-made avoid being hated by the Fear-driven? Because no one can hide what they are. What they see to hate is the wordless initial processing of *existential information,* regardless of whether we attempt to appease them. They know that what they said or did was picked up by our perceptiveness—that we *know* and are willing to *see.* We conveyed to them in that moment that we are not fundamentally afraid of *life,* regardless of any other neurotic problems we may have yet to overcome. If we try to fit in, they see us as the most offensive of all posers. We unknowingly mock them by trying to hide the two values their view of existence makes impossible: power and certainty. They recognize an independent man immediately, reserving an insidious hatred for anyone who doesn't practice their all-excusing virtue: the all-accepting, undemanding approximation of existence and consciousness. They know that *reality is real* for us—that life is real for us—and *that* is what they cannot forgive. The Self-made will always have one or many in a group take a strong, malicious dislike for him without ever speaking a word. His very existence is an affront to them—the upright posture, the steady, scrutinizing gaze, the arrogant smile, the untroubled forehead and youthful vitality—it all adds up to the only passionate response you can expect to see from a Spirit Murderer—the evasion clouded desire to kill.

We will conflict with anyone who isn't Self-made to the extent they are not, in any realm of their lives. Once again, we may try to excuse them by claiming *"they know not what they do,"* but one must identify a thing's nature to except or reject it. To say "No!"—to intentionally reject the good—is to *understand.*

Warrior Note: *We must be as ruthless about virtue as they are about evil.*

They want revenge; not for a moral failure, but for a lack of moral failure. The motives accused, are actually the motives of the accusers. No longer will they get away with blaming the victim. There will be no more plea-bargaining of our spirits through falsely admitted guilt.

The truth is, Spirit Murderers are powerless; *we* provide the fuel to make their premises work. Don't kid yourself into passivity though, because they will keep coming. Remember the Self-made tenet that *all* knowledge is a blessing, and be ready to use it when things are at their worst. Fake nothing for Spirit Murderers, or they will reform the very life out of you.

They want a buffer between themselves and thought, between their actions and their consequences. You *are* that buffer. Respecting no boundaries between men is not an offshoot of brotherly love, but of burglary, whether the victims are willing or not. Jails take people who cannot coexist civilly, out of circulation. Immoral beings likewise, if only in your personal awareness, must be confined to the contexts where they can do no harm to you and yours. We must fight their resistance to life and living patterns. We can no longer permit the simple fact of being human to be damned. To them I say, "*You can learn from us or you can try to kill us, but there is no other course to take. We now have the moral clarity we needed; we have the steady eyes to pin you right to the wall. We know what you are doing. Surrender or die.*"

Chapter Six

The Principles of Enduring Freedom

"[O]ur fathers brought forth on this continent, a new nation, conceived in liberty, and dedicated to the proposition that all men are created equal.
Now we are engaged in a great civil war, testing whether that nation, or any nation so conceived and so dedicated, can long endure." -Abraham Lincoln

Part of American reflection is as witness to the ebb and flow of sound principles in our society. As a people, we revolted violently against tyranny; a righteous stand fought with fatal resolve and the moral certainty of our just course. With victory, we watched America grow wealthy and safe, but time buried the links between our original stand and the ill traits of men that require eternal vigilance.

Whenever we have let our guard down, evil clamps on to foment a new crisis; it is a seemingly never-ending cycle. Our often-chaotic response reveals the uncertainty and decay of our principles; yet just as seasons change, vitality can be renewed as our moral awareness and control is reestablished. Without the proper moral armor, such waves of corruption will surely crash over us again, challenging our stand until the end of time.

If we held our deepest values as a part of our daily awareness, we could greatly lessen the approaching storms. We don't have to focus on the darkening skies. With dreams, goals and ideals in front of us, we will be instantly aware of all things contrary. Let's take a look at the most influential realms of human action; the pinnacle realms who's posture reveals whether our sacred freedoms are in jeopardy, or on track to endure any hardship.

The Arts

We see the most moral controversy in the subject of art and entertainment, and rightly so. It is hard to describe the reactions we have to it, but our artistic likes and dislikes are very important. They show how we feel about human beings and how we feel about our world. What we all prefer in art indicates the future advance or decline of America, and how quickly we can change things.

Everyone's life should feel like a work of art. Those who seek fulfillment by achieving the best within themselves will wish to experience and express it through every physical sense and their guiding power: our deepest understanding and emotions. We need to bring the deepest meaning of our lives as well as our most passionate expression towards it into our immediate awareness. Since our pursuit of values is lifelong, we need regular spans of time where we can experience a sense of completion—the reward of our values having been achieved. Romantic art satisfies this desire. What is truly ideal? What *should* we be? What is worth working for and striving towards? Romanticism is a sanctuary for the best within us—where the results of our effort are loved, encouraged, and fostered. Such art *gratifies* living effort, stylizing every facet of Man and of existence, every kind of thought, every shade of emotion, every shape of detail, and the grace in action of all living things.

A romantic artist shares the reward of his own mental state, revealing his deepest view of our stature and our environment. What he chooses to present in colors, in landscape, in words, in musical harmony, or in form, is what he finds most significant. To the extent that an artist is rational, his work will reflect living values. His style will reflect his intelligence and his skill will reveal the effort he brings to achieve his values.

An *irrational* artist will be just as passionate about destroying values as we are about enjoying them. History is littered with the distortions of those at odds with existence in every artistic medium. They corrupt beauty, purpose, and discipline in preference to the repulsive, the aimless, and the indefinable. Such artists are made popular by their spiritual equivalents and are tolerated by the rest of us through moral confusion.

Parents have been concerned for eons about the effect rock stars and movie heroes have on our children, and they are right to be concerned. What kids are shown gives them alternatives they wouldn't otherwise have had, and they can be constructive or destructive. We need to be aware of its moral impact—be it a movie, a video game, or a CD—to counter or underscore its influence. That understanding also reveals the integrity of the businessmen behind the product. It is fascinating to see the exact moral countenance of those whose work you are observing. By acquiring it, when you encounter offensive nonsense, you will never be speechless in this regard again.

Those conscious of the virtue in their own lifestyles can remain aware of this artistic link at all times, allowing romanticism to accent their every endeavor. This fulfillment can be enjoyed any time you look to see that your choices are *the right* choices. *All* human ideals have artistic value and emit a sense of glamour; and if you stay true to them, you *deserve* to bask in the light of this most precious reward.

Sound Institutions

In a speech, Abraham Lincoln said "So far as possible, the people everywhere shall have that sense of perfect security, which is most favorable to calm thought and reflection." This is the highest goal of Self-made Man; true peace on Earth. It has never been clear however, just what this goal rests upon.

Sound institutions are built upon sound relationships, which are built upon sound cognition. All Self-made organizations share the same value structure, as they are all designed by the same kind of mind. Productive groups who bring freedom, peace, and bounty to men are the foundation of a civilization. Self-made business and political leaders see the greatest power in truth; being open, honest, and fully accountable for their activities. They seek voluntary exchanges and enter negotiations with their own backbones, prepared to satisfy the terms agreed on. They put their best foot forward as goodwill requires, intending to leave a healthy impression as their only means to secure future association. Decency requires us all to accept the vulnerability of not controlling the others involved. The Self-made enjoy the opportunity of a free market environment, as fixed rewards draw only yawns from enterprising men.

Stand face to face with one other human being, and realize that trust—the integrity that you both respect and intend to live by a civil order—is all you have between you. In order to function socially, we must be completely free of concern for any threat to our lives or any forcible loss. Add another person, and trust is all you have. Add five hundred, and honesty, rationality, and integrity continues to be your guide. Add fifty million, and all that guarantees the character of men and keeps everyone from backing into corners, is trust. To trust is to feel comfortable about the actions and potential actions of others, and that only comes with a clear pattern of cognition acknowledged by all as moral, to which *every aspect* of human existence and our interrelation is gauged—be it law, business, education, or any other institution Man might form.

All the activities of Man are comprehendible by the rest. Even the running of a business empire or a country has base essentials that anyone can understand. The heights we can rise to are determined by a civilization's respect for the rights of the individual. This is why America has done so well relative to the rest of the world—why it has brought more wealth into the hands of more people than any other system of government. Our prosperity stems from the philosophy we hold. With an even greater moral clarity in the hands of the masses, our future will contain more positive manifestations than I could possibly predict, and I look forward to witnessing them.

Philosophy

In our history, most philosophers spent their time building useless theories and refuting others, often generating nothing new. The field was created by the passionate (Aristotle), heightened by the learned (St. Thomas Aquinas, our Founding Fathers, Ayn Rand), and ran into the ground by the malicious (Kant, Sartre, Marx). But all quietly performed revolutions in an era's thought, not necessarily for the better. It is time to bring philosophy back to its proper stature, as its effect on mankind is staggering.

A host of men throughout history have been declared philosophers, while their thinking consisted of claiming that Man cannot think. From Plato's *"We know that we know nothing,"* to Sartre's *"My existence is absurd"* (that was true by the way), a long line—Hegel, Marx, Kant, Hume—have been some of the world's most influential minds. Modern professors jump on the bandwagon, enjoying the spectacle of leaving their students speechless in response to unanswerable questions, declaring the futility of the mind and its sensate capacities. But the title of "intellectual" can only be granted to those who show discipline in the use of their intellect, not to those who *evade* its use.

Such men have given the field of philosophy the air of unprofessionalism it now has. Aristotle's every action implied that philosophy was for practical use; not the province for senseless utopias. Most others used their minds to question whether or not the mind was of any use, and the wise, to their credit, dismissed them. Unfortunately, the whole field of philosophy was tainted through cultural expulsion, prompted by those seeking sound, useful, and intelligent moral guidance. The phonies removed science from philosophy, which made religion almost appealing by comparison.

A mathematician doesn't question whether or not humans can add. No endeavors of Man are ever to question whether or not we have any capacity to investigate them, if they are to be considered scientific, philosophical, or rational. To close the issue once and for all, *if you want to argue against the validity of Man's senses, you will have to—in good faith—figure out a way to convey your stand to me without using them.*

With this work, I hope to return philosophy to its proper role in education—that of coherently guiding Man to fulfillment in every aspect of his existence. Marx claimed that the essential division between men was economic. I say the essential classes of men are defined by the base premise that drives their consciousness, and that all motives stem from within a man himself. A rational philosophy for living integrates *every single thing you know,* giving clear classification and clear links to where every bit of knowledge is coming from and going to. There is no limit to its usefulness, and with moral awareness of its value, we can become not just spiritually fulfilled, but spiritually *self-sufficient* as well.

Freeing Education

"How do you explain school to higher intelligence?" —E.T.

As a student grows, he discovers that teachers already have opinions about his subjects of interest and have a system in place, not to help him live an unlimited progression, but to confine him and his ambition. His authorities negate his competence, take his inspiration, and tell him what it has to be and who it has to serve. If he accepts it, the student's sense of discovery wanes and is bent to learning the laws of men and their constraints.

Such teachers fear the renegade who ignores social boundaries in his upward surge—America's eternal hero—and they should. A well-rounded education is not the *cause* of prosperity, but the *result* of pursuing an individual purpose. Individual purpose is a topic requiring courage however, and in this environment, is quickly substituted with an esteem vacuum: the lifeless void of social conformity.

Grade School

Often, our schools grade on curves instead of assuring competence. They pander to self-esteem instead of instilling *the cause* of self-esteem, a folly the outside world will never cater to. Their psychologists tell us that kids aren't just unruly these days, they are *sick*. They have this disease or that disorder; it couldn't be that they are *kids*. They have to be labeled, drugged, and told there is something wrong with them—a burden they carry for life. Ironically, this coincides with a Cold War Communist infiltration plan called *Psychopolitics*. Be they Cold War machinations or not, psychology is a weak science, littered with fraud, poorly thought out and poorly validated claims, which has been hijacked by pharmaceutical companies eager to exploit a new market. Read the latest DSM and you will see them recommending drugs to infants for supposed mental disorders. Infants? This is based on *biomarkers;* a highly questionable method of diagnosis. Claimed "treatable maladies" have expanded like a cancer, and they have set the bar so low—pacing the normal ups and downs of day-to-day life—that everyone can be considered crazy now. This is preposterous: in some cases driven by morons who pine for their ramblings to be significant, and in others, by hegemonic forces wanting control over America's future and lifelong drug customers as gravy. Dumbing kids down and racking their bodies with drugs, such approaches pattern grade school more and more, not for independence after graduation, but as if the students will be going on welfare.

In part, the ineffectiveness of public schools stems from their disassociation with the profit motive. Private schools *have* to be good. Public schools are funded regardless, leaving the system free to degenerate in countless ways, including the vulnerability of dark control by elitists hostile to any new crops of free-thinking independence in those they consider "peasant" children. Welcome to the limitations of the future.

I agree with Benjamin Franklin that all citizens should be educated at least to the degree necessary to function in society, and that it serves them beyond all doubt. To assure living competence to all, public schools must maintain competitive standards of excellence and teachers should be paid by merit. While home schooling is growing in popularity (and for good reason), if you are proven to be a good teacher for your own kids, every such parent should be in front of a private classroom for specific subjects; otherwise, it is a senseless duplication of effort. Besides, kids need social skills: experience dealing with a wide variety of personality types and ages; certainly their own. We learn a lot from other kids in watching and experiencing their attributes—good and bad; something Mom and Dad can't help us with. There are certainly troubling influences in the world, but there are many splendid forces as well, and kids need exposure to both so they can tell the difference and learn how to protect themselves from evil. On the public side, if schools hope to retain students, Mom and Dad deserve a regular vote regarding what is taught in schools, how it is taught, and what influences are permitted on school grounds.

Note to parents: If schools want to force drugs on your child for supposed disorders, including vaccines, get them out. If your child exhibits actual behavioral issues, get a blood test immediately and look for heavy metal poisoning. If the school is not focused on reading (self-generated comprehension), writing (self-expression), arithmetic (effective calculation), and the physical sciences (practical applications of thought and action), the child's independence is at risk. Supplement their education at the very least. Proper education must address the fundamentals so the mind can operate without falsely imposed limits: cognitive structure before content, cognitive efficiency and discipline before emotional indulgence.

Note to young adults: Your parents know how hard it is to survive, and it is only getting harder. Dependent kids (those not paying for food or a place to stay) lack the mindset to judge this; only independent individuals can grasp it fully. It is a parent's job to help provide the tools you need to launch your life right. Time is critical, and if you are wasting it on non-productive endeavors (anything that is not personal advancement, skill-honing, and career-minded) and/or are treating your parents poorly, frustrating them and their sense of urgency, you may find yourself out on the street. Benjamin Franklin threw his best friend right out of the boat when he wouldn't row. No one has time or energy anymore to tolerate those who won't focus and contribute. Take the goal of independence seriously (and the effort necessary to achieve it) or you may be next.

College

Unfortunately, the excruciating cost of a college education looks more like indentured servitude than a route to a better life for students these days. Student loans are stretching into their *retirement* now! It has gotten out of scale with what graduates can expect to earn in many fields (such as teaching), and has instigated a further division of social classes as a result. Personally, I believe this is intentional: a weight upon the middle class under which the children of the wealthy are immune. We studied the rapid increases in tuition over the last 20 years in a finance class and found no logical link to costs—no justification for a rise of almost 300%—no concern over what it does to the kids, their parents, or the economy—just the pursuit of maximum profit. Once a bastion of culture and refinement, higher education has become a racket that should be boycotted. Great ideas are abound however, from no interest, tax-deductible loans to free, state-provided degree programs; let's make one or more of them stick. Here is another: have all professors become accredited free agents, collecting class fees, holding classes wherever they find reasonable room rates, and paying universities a sensible administration fee for structuring degree programs for students and verifying all requirements are met. If we don't hold the cost of education in check, formal degree programs will soon be out of reach for most young people, and the disruption in availability of quality schooling for ALL of our children will hasten America's downward spiral.

Of course, higher learning is *always* within reach if you seek it yourself. Education is intended to prepare you for self-sustenance at the highest level you care to achieve, and you can acquire that knowledge on your own. For those seeking alternative resources, the self-help genre has answers for everyone, making it a lot easier for the teacher to be in the right place at the right time. Self-made Man seeks knowledge wherever he can find it. The best in each field were my teachers, through authorship—American presidents and statesmen, psychologists, philosophers, and businessmen. There are great books written on every topic; great seminars, audio-programs, and workshops designed to ingrain very specific skills, which you can walk out of the classroom with and use today. Often the best realize the value of their ability, and *thank pride,* they write it down. Warren Buffet, Ricardo Semler, Ayn Rand, Donald Trump—all deserve the highest praise for leaving us evidence of so many remarkable minds. How wonderful it is to be so entranced by one's teacher.

I found instructors who teach *and* work in their fields and took their classes. I found a mix of theory and practicality worked best for me—an apprenticeship education similar to that found in Europe, tailored to my interests alone along paths that were commercially viable.

Such an education has cost no less—probably more as it has become a lifelong pursuit—but my conscience is clear; none of my time has been wasted and no false patterns, such as cramming and forgetting, were ingrained. Having taken control of my own education, it is hard to convey the immense pleasure I get from learning now. Learning is an adventure. Discovery is fascinating—out in the world and within my own mind.

I sympathize with the self-educated as they are often denied opportunities which are handed to the degreed, regardless of comparable ability. Our culture shouldn't confuse the un-degreed with the unprofessional, as the world has an overwhelming percentage of self-taught, self-made millionaires. After all, it wasn't Dr. Aristotle, Dr. Thomas Edison, or Dr. Jesus. What are *anyone's* credentials once they are working? *Results;* and actually, true credentials have never been anything else. Life is an education you never graduate from, giving us a chain of knowledge longer and more useful than any university could provide. If we are not stuck in a rut of repetition, we are building a very potent body of life-furthering knowledge—a wealth to be proud of. Regarding the question *"Do you have a degree?"* my response has always been *"I have the degree of intelligence necessary to perform the work I'm interviewing for, and I'll be glad to prove it."* More often than not, I have been given the chance. Not all economies offer that opportunity, however.

In the Great Recession, so many people were thrown out of work that companies hiring had to restrict applications to the degreed only, which cut the numbers standing at the gate from 1000 to ten. It is horrible to be out of work, but imagine the overwhelm on the other side as well when they have only one job opening. When I found myself on the wrong side of the gate, I went back to school. With project management experience, I was able to get my bachelor's degree faster than anyone I had ever known, and much more cheaply. I wrote an eBook about it to help others in the same situation, titled

Bachelor Monkey!

Swing a Four-Year College Degree in One Year without Going Bananas!

Visit BachelorMonkey.com or FastDegreeSystems.com to view the project. Follow suit if you haven't finished school yet, and you will have the degree as a backup, rather than regrets if times turn against you. If you are paying the college tuition for your kids or grandkids, *Bachelor Monkey!* will save *you* thousands and *them* a lot of time and agony. Extra tip from a dip: let the company who hires you pay for your Master's.

We must invest in education if we want America to be the envy of the world once more. At one time, our leaders had the vision to see generations ahead, and knew what that investment would yield; one of the most advanced civilizations in history. We need the honor of that vision again.

Freedom of Speech and Expression

As an "American POW" during George W. Bush's term in office, I became afraid to speak out. I was hesitant to openly question during media appearances, the many ominous developments in our country. The expansion of covert personnel under Homeland Security was unprecedented, to where even small hometown discussion groups were "infiltrated". As Bush said, *"If you're not with us, you're against us"* – a typical submission/ domination mindset which leaves little room for dissenting opinion. Being held without cause indefinitely for a cryptic and indefensible "terror" charge is enough to silence anyone.

Since 9/11, I have watched TV guest experts vehemently attacked for questioning the official version of events. The press reacted the same after the Kennedy assassination. If an expert probes for clarity, demonstrates a violation of physics, or looks into the backgrounds of those held responsible or those who benefitted most, commentators cut them off immediately and launch into a string of insults and ridicule. This made me very uneasy, as only guilty men respond this way. They must know where the questions ultimately lead, so they sidestep by implying that it is *absurd* and unpatriotic to raise the possibility that crimes could be committed by *any* of our saintly public representatives.

Such commentators don't weigh the facts and draw conclusions as responsible men would. They operate the Spirit Murdering pattern of evasion and destructive action, attempting to impose their will on the populace and writing off any carefully deliberating mind as a conspiracy nut or a whack job. A conspiracy is nothing more than two or more individuals planning to commit a crime. Conspiracies can happen at any level; from a bank robber and getaway driver, to a $50 billion ponzi scheme with regulators paid to look the other way, to the black-ops demolishing of a skyscraper. If you encounter those in important positions who refuse to acknowledge and chase down all available leads, then steady your aim and let the chips fall where they may: you have found someone who is in some way involved.

Free speech is a critical check to illegitimate power. While three branches share the power of administration, the trunk is the people, and free speech is the foundation on which their power rests. Its exercise is critical in the realm of major media, particularly when the major media is tasked with disseminating the government's stand on affairs. The people must be able to answer with a bullhorn of the same magnitude. Our citizen's representatives used to take the form of investigative reporters, but they have all but vanished from modern media today.

Free and Open Research, Investigations, and Reporting

We as a people must honor free speech above all and its political check, investigative reporting. There is a war on independent research at present, due to the heavy level of covert action attempting to sway mass sentiment, and the need to cover it up. Independent investigators are heroes for truth. They perform a dangerous job for minute compensation, fighting for justice, fairness, our safety and health—all that is right for a patriot and a decent human being to pursue. They are acutely aware of the long-term consequences from taking the easy way out—accepting lies and inaction when deep investigation and strong protest is called for. They act to raise awareness as our first line of defense against evil, and persist as a thorn in the side of the guilty. America must earn the right to say "We honor and protect our seekers." We have a peaceful, wholesome world to gain from their brave effort, with only the risk of acknowledgement on our part. They risk it all.

When enough evidence is gathered, we need citizen panels with subpoena authority should the court justices be compromised. When significant laws are passed to protect the people, they are quickly circumvented by the corrupt rich who have unlimited time and money available to undermine public intent. We need untapped resources to match. What if we utilized the wisdom we have sitting idle in retirement homes all over the country? Give those able among our learned elders the grand purpose of becoming investigators and researchers, guarding the American republic from high profile crimes and exposing those who commit them.

Lastly, any pertinent information uncovered needs to reach reporters with the courage to act on it. Unfortunately, most in today's lame-stream media are compromised. Too often, we have seen their evasive commentary: news anchors paid NOT to know why, confounded by the obvious, unable to ask hard questions or reach any logical conclusions. Some are naturals at it. Others are victims themselves; held hostage by their career disillusionment. Look at their dilemma: those who thrive on lies are elevated quickly and compensated well. Those of integrity who hesitate are threatened with job loss or outright career destruction. So what choice is left to them? Most journalists capitulate and say what they are told to say, avoid what they are told to avoid, write what they are told to write about, and defend what they are told to defend—and those watching can smell it. Free speech for the commentator, an American moral imperative, no longer exists. All such commentators today should start off by shrugging and saying, *"This is what my boss told me to say."*

Imagine being a journalist in the honorable, original sense—a crusader for truth—loving the creative process, finding the missing pieces, offering clarity, writing and speaking eloquently as a beacon of hope for all those you reach. Then see the gatekeepers to your dream penalizing you for every attribute that makes your chosen life and career worthwhile. If you insist on reporting the news unfiltered, you see yourself quickly run out of your field as the five media companies left in America all know the dangers of an honest man. Still, while the corrupt rich fight to consolidate the carcass of a media no longer trusted, alternatives are cropping up. Free voices are going independent through blogging and Internet radio. Their audiences are growing as the unfiltered truth and dealing in subjects with no boundaries resonates with an interest no censored commercial media source can compete with.

The censors are not the masters of your fate, *you are.* Reclaim your moral role in America and shine like you were meant to.

Free the Media

Before the 2012 presidential election, I researched Clear Channel, the largest radio station owner in the country, to determine the boundaries of what I could say on the air. All of the sudden Bain Capital popped up. It turned out that Mitt Romney's company *owned* Clear Channel during his presidential run. Coincidence? I had thought the glowing reports radio stations gave on Romney's campaign were humorously odd, while they downplayed President Obama's. Now it made sense. Unsurprisingly, I have never heard *any* form of media mention this conflict of interest.

Oftentimes, if you want a more honest perspective of what is going on in the world or even within the United States, you have to go to a foreign news service. There are two elements here: the gathering of the information itself, and its dissemination. The information source is just as important as the means of sharing. If there is a single organized source, the information can be real or manufactured. Pertinent information that could have drastically affected public reaction can be left out entirely. The result is that we know only what the source wants us to know; whatever steers us toward the conclusion they intend us to draw. For this reason, we must minimize information filters, let the bits come in, disseminate them raw, and draw conclusions as an informed populace once all available data is gathered. To assure legitimacy, nothing beats uncontrolled, independent sources.

Today, everything is predigested: conclusions are drawn for us, leaving us not the respectful role of mature contemplation and decision-making, but resistance to the decisions made as our only alternative. This is an affront to a sound republic, as a sound republic requires our involvement at the decision-making level. But information is power, and the Fear-driven never seek to share power. The Bible is a perfect example. The populace was left in the dark, vulnerable to the interpretation of those in control. No one knew what the text contained except a privileged few, who were then the sole authorities gauging moral adherence, able to control the conduct of the masses. Those who wish to build media empires must structure their enterprises to assure they do not disrupt the free flow of ideas; the risk to our freedom is just too great.

American media has undergone a massive consolidation since the 1980's, from over 50 companies to just five owners who control 96% of the America's information flow. In the 1940s, the banking monopoly admitted having total control over the media when they attempted to replace Roosevelt in a coup (see the congressional record). Legislation has gone back and forth over the years to regulate or deregulate ownership, and the thieving rich are winning. This consolidation by a few groups at the top, whether by open government decree or private means, reflects state ownership of the media. They control all dissemination and decide everything we know.

Media prices escalate when there are few avenues to turn to. Small voices are barred. They favor large advertisers and government agendas over the good of the people. They stop citizens groups from advertising if the message of the people conflicts with their own. They can easily blacklist authors, artists, and professionals who offer viewpoints they don't want the public to hear. They protect affiliated politicians and keep hard questions and scrutiny from ever reaching them. One central message syndicated nationally sounds efficient until you raise the question of whose voice it will be. We must encourage diversity in media, not discourage it.

With a few rules in place to protect a free press, monopolies on information and its dissemination can become endangered species:

1. No media group may own or control more than 25% of a local market.
2. No media group may own or control more than 5% of the national market.
3. No government entity, intelligence service, or affiliate may act as a sole source of information regarding foreign or domestic matters.
4. All retractions must be printed in the same size font as the original story (headline and text) on the front page.

The greatest men human history has to offer—Thomas Jefferson, John Hancock, Benjamin Franklin, Abraham

Lincoln, Thomas Edison—were well attuned to the machinations of the thieving rich. All fiercely opposed the evergreen conspiracy in finance, which in our time has taken the name of *Federal Reserve*; another topic considered "absurd" and off-limits today. My fellow Americans: when it comes down to it, whom are you going to trust, the giants of our past? Or the modern-day media inquisitors with faked popularity ratings? We are being conditioned that it is not intelligent to question the conclusions prepared for us; that it is foolish to disagree; that it is not patriotic to *think for ourselves*. If a sneering commentator bars free and thoughtful deliberation, then we, as responsible, *truly* patriotic Americans, need to inundate them with calls and/or *boycott* the network until such people are removed and the network's "news" and commentary becomes honest and wholesome again.

Nothing threatens the prevailing order more than access to the information we need to make decisions. Whoever controls information controls the outcome. The Fear-driven's mortal enemy in all cases is free will. So let's free Willy! End the media monopoly. End their ability to cover things up and our risk of being victimized by high profile crimes will drop dramatically.

Free the Medical Field!

Spirit Murderers are firmly in control of America's health. Some of their most atrocious actions against the populace are focused on children, whose long-term impacts have been left unstudied. Unsuspecting parents, doing what they've been told is right for their children, could in many cases be causing them irreparable harm, lifelong sickness, infertility, and an early death; just what a Spirit Murderer would want for us all.

Ending the Reign of Vaccines

"Vaccination is a barbarous practice and one of the most fatal of all the delusions current in our time." —Gandhi

Vaccines are often credited with having wiped out countless diseases, but the most widespread diseases were in considerable decline prior to their introduction. This was due to improved environmental conditions: clean water, better sanitation practices, and better food, but claiming the hero was vaccines makes a better story; one corrupt men could build an industry on. Contrary to the 'vaccine as savior' argument, long-term studies by MD's have found childhood illnesses such as measles, mumps, and rubella can prevent serious adult diseases, such as heart attack, stroke, allergies, and cancer, later on. The illnesses themselves create deeper immunities, which are then lacking in those vaccinated. Believe it or not, no studies have been done by the CDC/FDA regarding the ongoing health of vaccinated kids versus those unvaccinated. But private studies have been done: vaccinated kids show highly elevated susceptibilities to chronic illness versus unvaccinated kids—by over 30%—due to compromised immune systems and exposure to countless pathogens within the vaccines themselves.

People think vaccination equates to immunity. Not true. Whole groups of vaccinated people have died from the very diseases they were supposedly protected against. Such was the experience in India during smallpox outbreaks. Gandhi recognized vaccination as a means of Western control, which capitalizes on our fear of disease but is unsafe and ineffective at its declared purpose, but rather effective at *spreading* disease, intentionally or otherwise.

Read the label on any vaccine and understand how risky a proposition it is. For a society that more and more seeks natural, organic ingredients, vaccine labels read like Nazi Death Camp Cocktails: Thimerosal/Mercury (Poison), Polysorbate 80 (Cancer), Phenol (Toxic), MSG (Neurotoxin), Neomycin (Allergen), Squalene (Gulf War Syndrome and now flu vaccines), Aluminum (Alzheimers/Neurotoxin that can amplify the toxicity of mercury by 100 times), Ammonium Sulfate (Poison), Parasites (Viri and Bacteria), Formaldehyde/Formalin (Poison that along with aluminum increases toxic yield of mercury 1000 times), Glutaraldehyde (Birth Defects), Beta-Propiolactone (Cancer/ Poison), and many others strained through animal and human matter that may be contaminated with herpes and other alarming pathogens, which can damage DNA and cause severe auto-immune reactions.

Now, take this beautiful newborn baby and inject all of the worst filth he or she could ever come across in life—all of the industrial poisons, dreaded diseases, and deadliest viruses in history, strained through putrefied, disease-ridden tissue—all at once, and somehow he will be healthier? The toxicologist, Dr. Boyd Haley, considered even one vaccine to be too much for an infant to handle: *"A single vaccine given to a six-pound newborn is the equivalent of giving a 180-pound adult 30 vaccinations on the same day."* In 1975, Japan stopped vaccinating kids under two years old and saw their infant mortality rates plummet to be the best in the world. They have reversed course since, likely due to pressure from the US whose infant mortality rate was #33 on the list of countries by comparison. While in the US, two parts mercury per billion is allowed in drinking water, vaccines may contain 51,000 parts per billion of mercury (davidicke.com), and mercury poisoning directly reflects symptoms of autism.

"As it turns out, we are injecting our children with 400 times the amount of mercury that the FDA or EPA considers safe."
-Robert F. Kennedy, Jr.

So what if the unbearable happens: you indulge your doctor, permit vaccination, and your perfectly healthy child suddenly loses all animation, conscious composure, eye control, and motor skills?

In a normal injury case, parents have the right to sue who wronged their child in a public trial with a judge, jury, attorneys, legal precedent to rely on, and proper discovery for the exploration of all evidence. With vaccine injuries however, pharmaceutical lobbies have bought the entire legal process. The 1986 National Childhood Vaccine Injury Act, shields, not children from bad vaccines, but vaccine administrators and manufacturers from you. Parents cannot sue. They have to petition the US Department of Health and Human Services to get a ruling on whether any compensation is justified. American taxpayers foot the bill for legal representation on both sides and pay for any awarded compensation. Parents have difficulty getting any legal help at all as the DHHS is notorious for cutting plaintiff lawyer fees and making them wait a decade or more to be paid. The pharmaceutical companies at fault pay nothing, don't have to show up, and *are not* required to disclose any data. The public is not allowed to witness the hearings; neither are reporters. There is no judge or jury, but an administrator appointed with sole responsibility to hear the case and decide. Meanwhile, the DHHS holds patents on the very vaccines they are hearing cases on, and are paid handsomely by the pharmaceutical companies who manufacture them; another pathetic conflict of interest.

So what happened after drug lobbyists got this law passed? Massive increases in the number of vaccines as there is no longer any risk to pharmaceutical companies. Sixty-nine doses of 16 vaccines for every child are now recommended by the CDC, yet NO studies have been done of the long-term effects of the vaccines. NO studies have been done of multiple vaccines administered together! NO studies have been done to determine the effect of the entire vaccination schedule. This is bad science at best, and at worst, a key branch of a depopulation agenda. Prior to the passing of this law, diagnosis of autism was 1 in 10,000 kids born. Now it is 1 in 50. *Half* of all American children now suffer from chronic disease and disabilities.

Because of the law, the field is an immoral free for all. Several CDC studies are found to have been subject to data manipulation to bury the clear vaccine/autism link (Verstraeten/De-Stefano studies found a 340% correlation) and keep the money flowing. Testing is conducted by agencies with conflicts of interest but not against inert placebos, so there is no objectivity. Personnel are allowed entrepreneurial reign over their own concoctions; developing, testing, authorizing them for use, and becoming wealthy from their sale. Environmental activist and attorney Robert F. Kennedy Jr. described the *"CDC as a cesspool of corruption, mismanagement and dysfunction with alarming conflicts of interest suborning its research, regulatory and policymaking functions."* People? Wake up: the threat is real.

"When injustice becomes law, resistance becomes duty."
—Thomas Jefferson

Vaccinations are like bad plastic surgery; it seems like a good idea until we become caricatures of ourselves, unnatural refuse of an outmoded technology, realizing our knee-jerk reaction to do something to protect our kids overrode the fact that our solution was not sound, healthy, or even safe. Nothing could match the infamy of seeing our most cherished creations shattered by those we thought we could trust; those who preyed on our fear and irreparably damaged our lives, having stolen our children from us, and our children's futures from them. Don't risk destroying your child with these poison cocktails. Don't wait for a callous pediatrician to tell you *"It's just a coincidence that your child came in healthy and left with permanent brain damage. You have no right to question me. I am a doctor, superior to everyone. I tell you what to do, you do it, and if a problem arises, you are on your own. I am NOT liable; please leave and find another doctor. Here is an autism pamphlet. Good day."* Attempt a public outcry and we watch the television commentator's snide persona descend upon them as it is the media's job to mock, insult, and ridicule grieving parents and conscientious MD's who ask hard questions. Watch who the media and doctors protect. If the children are not their first concern, you know what to think of them.

Projections indicate it will soon be 1 in 4 children with autism. Parents are playing Russian roulette with a devastatingly corrupt system that has legal immunity. Just don't vaccinate. If in doubt, wait. Mimic Japan's results at least: no vaccinations before year two.

"To all the pediatricians in the world, please show me the study that found 69 doses of 16 vaccines do not cause cancer, auto-immune disease, and brain injury." –Dr. Jack Wolfson

No honest group seeks to isolate itself of all liability for its own actions. Honest groups are fully accountable, open to independent audit of all data and records, and committed to constant improvement. Dishonest groups seek protection to get away with anything; in this case, chemical warfare against helpless children. The moral abomination of incapacitating our youth has the power to steal America's future. Every family forced to deal with a lifelong dependent is another family economically sidetracked for life, and is no longer perceived as a threat. If any issue justifies a call to arms, it is this.

Would you really choose to inject your child with filth from the lowest street trash, teaming with every disease imaginable: hepatitis, herpes, HIV—products of the lowest judgment which your own child, due to a positive upbringing, would never likely encounter? This festering pollution in their bloodstream guarantees a lifetime of illness for your child and a corrupt health system a steady stream of business for life. Deny them this income, and this whole immoral approach to medicine. If you or your children have had vaccinations, you likely have heavy metal poisoning. You need intravenous chelation therapy to draw the heavy metals—mercury, lead, aluminum—out of your body and electronic zapping (more on that later) of any foreign pathogens that have come along for the ride.

Freedom from Cancer

Many years ago I was engaged to a wonderful girl. With her literature background, she became my copy editor, and we enjoyed a magical, romantic discourse over philosophy and the bright futures we were free to define and pursue. As time went on, due to our vibrant and varied interests, we had moved on to other life experiences, but we stayed close emotionally with the prospect of reuniting once our careers took shape and things settled down. It was not to be. One day she called to say she had cancer; she was stage four at diagnosis and they didn't tell her how long she had. I wanted to drop everything and look for a cure, but I was struggling not to drown myself due to the economic collapse. I told her what I knew, knowing she was every bit as capable to find the answers and solve this as I was. She bounced back well initially, then slowly began to deteriorate. After fighting for many years, she was talked into chemotherapy and I knew it was over. She slipped into a coma after a six-month quarantine following a bone marrow transplant and died three months later. I was devastated by this. My future was devastated by this. So I find myself manically researching cancer cures years later, still trying to save her.

What I've run into with cancer research is story after story of doctors doggedly harassed by the FDA for helping patients get better. The more promising their research and results, the more harassment they have suffered. Usually dismissed out of hand, when the evidence is unavoidable and finally acknowledged to justify pursuing trials, the FDA conducts them slipshod with blatant violations of the doctor's protocols to guarantee failure. Though statistics show a typical success rate between 80-90% with the doctor's unhampered treatments versus 2% for chemotherapy and radiation (and 2 of every 3 conventional patients dies within 5 years), subjects are often forced to endure the gauntlet of high-dollar toxic chemotherapy and radiation before they are even allowed to try alternatives. By then, their immune system is knocked down so severely, they are lucky to respond to anything.

If you or a loved one is suffering from cancer, here is a brief rundown of the therapies I have encountered and the prices paid by those who have pioneered their discovery:

Anti-neoplastons: 60% success rate. Dr. Stanislaw Burzynski is the first doctor ever to have cured brain cancer. He found that peptides and amino acids, which he termed anti-neoplastons, were present in the fluids of healthy people but absent in those with cancer. Reintroduction of the anti-neoplastons immediately reversed the progress of the cancer. He has been viciously attacked by the FDA/AMA/Texas Medical Board and sued continuously for twenty years, who have made repeated attempts to *steal his patents.* You can witness the atrocious conduct of the government and media in real time regarding Dr. Burzynski's cures today. Watch *Burzynski – The Movie* on YouTube. Clinic is in Houston, TX. Visit BurzynskiClinic.com.

GcMAF Immunotherapy: (Gc protein derived microphage activating factor). 90% success rate. Nagalase, an enzyme released by most cancers, keeps macrophages (large white blood cells) dormant. Glycoproteins are used to reawaken macrophages and jumpstart the immune system. Lots of people have been killed over this one. In 2015 alone, ten doctors in Florida researching GcMAF have gone missing or been murdered (I suspect they discovered the presence of nagalase in vaccines). GcMAF has the power to reverse the symptoms of autism (25-85% recovery rate), undoing all of the hard work the CDC has done to destroy our children. Restoring 20 immune responses in the body, GcMAF treats over 50 different diseases and 38 types of cancer. **Do it yourself:** GOleic food supplements have been developed and are available internationally online.

Visit: Immunocentre.eu
RenoIntegrativeMedicalCenter.com.

Rife Machines: 93% success rate. The sonic destruction of pathogens. Royal Rife, a microbiologist, invented the first high-magnification microscope. Scientists theorized about miniature worlds of microbes and viruses, but it was Royal Rife who showed this world to mankind. He also found that microbes resonated at certain sound frequencies, which if fed back to them, they could not withstand. He developed a frequency generator that could hone in on specific parasites and kill them, restoring the cells they invaded and supercharging the immune system. The AMA viciously attacked Royal Rife's work and he died penniless. **Do it yourself:** Frequency generators can be bought online, but are somewhat expensive ($3-5k) and most appropriate for those with advanced stages of disease. Visit NewHopeTechnologies.com for more information. Hulda Clark "Zappers" are more economical for do-it-yourself health maintenance.

Dr. Hulda Clark and *The Cure for All Diseases*: 95% success rate. Dr. Clark maintained that only two things were responsible for ill health: parasites and pollution, which often worked in tandem. Dr. Clark found a particular parasite recurring with *every major disease*. With cancer, the particular bug is Fasciolopsis Buskii, a flat worm. She developed a simple device called a zapper, which instantly kills parasites, bacteria, viruses, and molds in the bloodstream without needing to know their specific frequencies, and she treated cancer and other diseases with a combination of zapping, elimination of solvents and industrial pollution from the patient's body and environment, good nutrition, and digestive cleanses. Her work in many ways is the culmination of the best-known treatments, and offers the most extensively documented resources. Remarkably, Hulda Clark didn't attempt to patent anything; she gave away 100% of her research freely, teaching people to heal themselves better, with less pain, and for less money than can be done in the American medical system. **Do it yourself**: Critical and defiant of the medical profession's constant withholding of better methods, she laid out all of her protocols, printed diagrams of her electronic devices, and described her methods in her books in every detail. She offered the world a priceless level of independence from corrupt medicine, was attacked viciously for it and continues to be. Thank you Dr. Clark, for living by *"First, do no harm"*, and let her life be a lesson to practitioners who act more like lawyers than doctors today. Visit DrClarkStore.com. For a free download of *The Cure for All Diseases,* go to DrHuldaClark.org.

Essiac Tea: 73% success rate. A tea of four or more herbs known to kill cancer cells, centering on the sheep sorrel weed. Passed on to Rene Caisse in the 1920's, a nurse from Canada, and originally formulated by an Ojibway medicine man. Harassed by the Canadian Health Ministry during her 50 years of healing others. **Do it yourself:** formula available online and in books. Visit EssiacInfo.org.

Gerson Therapy: 100% success rate. Floods the body with nutrients from 15-20 pounds of organically grown fruits and vegetables daily; mostly in juice form. Liver detox/immune system boost with up to five coffee enemas per day. Max Gerson had considerable success with his therapy and endured lifelong harassment by organized medicine. Believed killed by Big Pharma via arsenic poisoning (though the AMA/FDA trend is one final insult: to claim the pioneers died of cancer). **Do it yourself:** protocols are online and in books. Clinic is in San Diego, CA. Visit Gerson.org.

Hoxsey Treatment: 80% success rate. Two herbal formulas, one internal and one external, using bloodroot and a host of herbs with potent anti-cancer properties, passed down by American Indians. Harry Hoxsey was arrested over 100 times during a spectacular 50-year battle with the AMA and FDA (who tried to buy his formulas), and ultimately moved his practice to Tijuana, Mexico. The Supreme Court and Congress found that organized medicine in the United States was a coercive monopoly that had conspired against Hoxsey, but the damage was done. **Do it yourself:** Herbs are listed on internet sites and in books. Visit HoxseyBiomedical.com.

Hyperthermia/Ablatherm Therapy: 50% success rate. Use of infrared, ultrasonic, radio wave, or radiating heat, locally or whole body, kills cancer cells and *liquefies* tumors. It was found by William Coley (of Coley's Toxins) that patients who developed a fever often went into remission. Approved for use by the FDA, though current pioneers are viciously attacked for their high success rates, particularly with prostate and breast cancer. **Do it yourself:** purpose built infrared heaters and lamps can be purchased for use at home.

Laetrile/Vitamin B17: 80% success rate. Apricot pit kernels have the highest concentration of vitamin B17 followed by peach pit kernels and the seeds of most berries. Available in Mexico in liquid IV form. Attacked by the FDA, which claims Laetrile to be toxic (it *is* toxic: to cancer). **Do it yourself:** crack open apricot pits to reveal a cancer killer. Follow online protocols for vitamin supplements and diet to maximize benefits. Plant a peach tree or buy kernels in bulk.

Oxygen Therapy/Ketogenic Diet: 80% success rate. As safe as breathing. Most of us breathe very shallow, and cancer cells thrive in a low oxygen environment. Using supplemental oxygen within a stimulated immune system can shrink tumors and get white blood cells doing their job again.

In 1931, biochemist Dr. Otto Warburg won the Nobel Prize for his research on cancer cells. He found that *"Cancer grows in oxygen-deprived, acidic tissue"*, and that cancer cells cannot survive in a highly oxygenated environment, adding that *"NO disease, including cancer, can exist in an alkaline environment"*, where a PH of 7.4 (slightly alkaline) is average for healthy cells. Further, he found that *"The prime cause of cancer is the replacement of the respiration of oxygen (oxidation of sugar) in normal body cells by fermentation of sugar."* As cancer cells have 23 or more glucose receptors compared to only two for a normal cell, this allows an uptake rate of 10-12x normal, rapidly accelerating tumor growth (so *sugar is the enemy*). *"All carcinogens impair respiration directly or indirectly by deranging capillary circulation. ... If ... exogenous carcinogens are excluded rigorously, then much of the endogenous cancer may be prevented today"*, an argument in strong favor of a low-carb, vegan diet. **Do it yourself:** Get outside as often as possible, deeply breathe fresh air. Hold several deep breaths and push to hyper-oxygenate your system (not to the point of passing out!). Walk. Get rid of all toxic chemicals in your house to improve air quality. Open windows to exchange air frequently. Don't consume things that rob you of oxygen (pop, alcohol, smoking, drugs, fluoride, exhaust/noxious fumes), and review *every* food and drink label to minimize sugar intake. Details on Warburg and the Ketogenic diet can be found at CharlieFoundation.org.

Ozone Therapy: 95% success rate. Extremely safe treatment as found by German and Russian doctors treating millions of patients. Enriches blood with oxygen through transfusion or IV. Viciously attacked and suppressed by the FDA. Administered by a health practitioner.

www.saisei-mirai.or.jp: fantastic Japanese clinic website for cutting edge cancer research, far from our laws, smear tactics, and suppression. Includes research papers and clinical data.

It isn't that we are on the verge of a cancer cure: we have had cures for over one hundred years. It is that we are coming to a point where the thieving rich can no longer stop them. There are many ways to go about curing cancer, all with success rates infinitely better than chemotherapy and radiation at a fraction of the price, and with no toxic or harmful side effects. Chemo and radiation have a downside: they kill you. These alternatives do not. Visit CancerActive.com and CancerTutor.com for more detailed information on a host of cancer cures.

The AMA and FDA are good 'ole boys clubs, owned and controlled by old money. They fight fiercely against all outsiders as a closed shop to preserve their control and pursue their own secret agendas rather than working for the interests of the people. There were two main factions in medicine: the natural healers and the empire builders. Carnegie, Rockefeller; men of great wealth but questionable integrity, created what they were good at: money machines: monopoly institutions—of learning, of certification, and of the medical press—and used them to control the education, thinking, and scope of work for doctors, penalizing all those who step outside the box. It has become a marketing system based on *high-profit continuity*, or disease management with pharmaceuticals, rather than cures, effectively driving out the pioneers and any approach that would have the patient stop spending money. In 1982, Dr. Richard Crout, Director of the FDA Bureau of Drugs, wrote:

"I never have and never will approve a new drug to an individual, but only to a large pharmaceutical firm with unlimited finances."

The following are excerpts from the infamous 1953 Fitzgerald Report, commissioned by the Senate Investigating Committee, which studied *"a Conspiracy against the Health of the American people"* in regard to independent cancer research, scientists/doctors, and treatment clinics.

"There is reason to believe that the AMA has been hasty, capricious, arbitrary, and outright dishonest ... the alleged

machinations of Dr. J. J. Moore (for the past ten years the treasurer of the AMA) could involve the AMA and others in an interstate conspiracy of alarming proportions."

"... this is the weirdest conglomeration of corrupt motives, intrigue, selfishness, jealousy, obstruction and conspiracy that I have ever seen."

"Dr. Fishbein [publisher of the AMA Journal] contended that the medicines employed by the Hoxsey Cancer Clinic had no therapeutic value; that it was run by a quack and a charlatan. ... Reprints and circulation of several million copies of articles so prepared resulted in litigation. ... Fishbein, who admitted that he had never practiced medicine one day in his life and had never had a private patient ... The jury ... concluded that Dr. Fishbein was wrong; that his published statements were false, and that the Hoxsey method of treating cancer did have therapeutic value."

"Dr. Reimann's report on cancer cases in Pennsylvania over a long period of time showed that those who received no treatment lived a longer period than those that received surgery, radium or x-ray. ... The survey also showed that following the use of radium and x-ray much more harm than good was done to the average cancer patient."

Regarding the Hoxsey clinic, *"The Council of National Cancer Institute ... sought in every way to hinder, suppress and restrict this institution in their treatment of cancer."*

"Existing agencies, both public and private, are engaged and have pursued a policy of harassment, ridicule, slander and libelous attacks on others sincerely engaged in stamping out this curse of mankind. ... a conspiracy does exist to stop the free flow and use of drugs in interstate commerce which allegedly has solid therapeutic value. Public and private funds have been thrown around like confetti at a country fair to close up and destroy clinics, hospitals and scientific research laboratories which do not conform to the viewpoint of medical associations. How long will the American people take this?"

"Should we sit idly by and count the number of physicians, surgeons and cancerologists who... because of fear or favor, are forced to line up with the ... American Medical Association"?

"it is but another manifestation of power and privilege of a few at the expense of the many would be more consistent with truth and wholly accurate."

As a testament to corrupt power, nothing was done. Independent clinical trials must be given the same legal standing as FDA trials. Their police power must be revoked, and we need an independent medical press for the same reason. They must be circumvented as an organization and the spirit of discovery and freedom to innovate restored to medicine as an American imperative. We need independent wealth sources–new wealth; internet wealth; uncorrupted wealth—to take responsibility for running professional trials that the FDA refuses to conduct. We need those with the financial wherewithal to fight legally and morally to the level the entrenched bureaucrats are capable of, digging into their lives and exposing their misdeeds just as loudly and thoroughly as they attack honest doctors and researchers. We need parallel organizations with no easily targeted center to nullify the power of our oppressors, whose results cannot be purchased or its guiding principles lobbied into mediocrity. In the future, when you hear "You have cancer", the emotional impact should be reduced to that of hearing "You have a cold", with a smorgasbord of cures readily available.

Decent doctors and researchers: please keep looking for cures and improving the ones found. Good people need your help and are cheering you on, even as the mercenaries of Big Pharma are targeting you. Carry guns. Shoot back.

Liberation from Heart Disease

Both of my parents had heart blockages. One chose angioplasty (stents), which temporarily relieves only those small areas, like unclogging a drain. The other asked for alternatives and was told of EDTA intravenous treatment (known as chelation therapy). This treatment removes calcium from the *entire* system, lowering the risk of stroke as well. Ethylenediaminetetraacetic acid (EDTA) was created by government scientists to combat lead poisoning in citizens due to painting warships in WW2. It binds with heavy metals and draws them out of the body. MD's of the time posited that it should help heart patients as well since the plaque in arteries is made up of calcium, which is a heavy metal. Curing heart disease however, is as popular with the sick rich as curing cancer, so doctors experimenting with EDTA have suffered the same scale of harassment and legal barriers from the same coercive monopolies.

For 50 years, EDTA has been the standard FDA approved treatment for heavy metal poisoning, but not for heart conditions. After 50 years of stonewalling, a $30 million double blind study proved EDTA effective in the treatment of heart disease, with up to a 50% reduction in cardiac events. Though it has wildly outstripped the efficacy of current treatments, the FDA continues to drag its feet with technical delays on implementation. Fortunately, oral supplements are available that can be taken daily to provide some level of protection. Intravenous care is also available by specialists.

The decision is yours. Spend $50,000 on heart surgery: it will slow down, alter, and limit your life forever and will not improve your lifespan. Or, spend $1,500 for EDTA chelation therapy: you will no longer need surgery and your living vibrancy can return, but the heart surgeon will not get his new Ferrari. He will have to go into another form of medicine or perhaps get a second job. The prestigious heart center will be foreclosed on instead of your home. You get to live a long time and die of natural causes.

For all major diseases in America, only the highest profit treatments are permitted by law, while their effectiveness is minimized to assure continuity of need.

Chemotherapy and radiation are so bad that NO treatment statistically results in a longer life span, and you can do nothing at all, FOR FREE. The grand buildings you see—cancer research centers, heart research centers—they are funded by the immense cost of treatment, and are a tribute, not to patients, but to the supposed "great" men who established the facility in the same spirit as kings building castles; a monument to themselves. In America's beginning, the modesty of our government structures was a moral spectacle in itself by contrast. Traditional cancer and heart disease treatments—the two biggest killers of Man—are approaching $1 trillion per year each. The income from all alternative therapies put together could not fund these developments, which is as it should be.

Warrior Note: *The suppression of cures (and the deliberate causing of illness) is health fraud, patient murder, and intent to commit murder. Like Nazi camp guards, try, convict, and execute those taking a conscious, active role.*

Chiropractors and the Freedom to Move

If you saw a wilted rose and noticed that its stem was broken, wouldn't you think *that* had something to do with it? In 1987, the American Medical Association was found guilty of conspiring to destroy the entire chiropractic field. They did this through their press and by educating new doctors to believe chiropractors were quacks and "unscientific cultists" who were immensely dangerous to their patients. Beginning in 1962, the AMA distributed

"Quack Packs" to all new students, which attacked the chiropractic profession from the outset. Young doctors were taught to ostracize and abandon patients who saw chiropractors, and never to associate with chiropractors at all, on a personal or professional level. Given the AMA/FDA's conduct regarding cures, you can see why they would be against chiropractic: inexpensive non-invasive treatment without drugs, no prospect for empire building, and no permanent dependencies.

Your spine is the core of your body, like the trunk of a tree. It carries and protects the nerves that send and receive signals directly from your brain, and those nerves cannot remain pinched without drastic consequences to the organs cut off from that vital link. All health emanates from this core, and a dislocated vertebra pinches a nerve like a garden hose. No flow, or greatly reduced flow, starves the organs it feeds. This was proven in 1921 by Henry Windsor, an MD who posited that dislocated vertebra led to organ disease and failure. He performed 75 human and 25 animal autopsies, and found a near 100% correlation: where an organ had failed, such as in lung disease or kidney disease, there was a subluxated vertebrae pinching off the organ, which led to the person's death. Studies conducted by other doctors over the following decades confirmed his conclusions. Proper spinal alignment offers pain-free motion, optimum organ function, maximum energy, and the clearest thinking. A recent study shows that a properly adjusted neck increases cognitive function by up to 20%!

It always made the most sense to me to try the least invasive treatments first, drugs second, and surgery last. Once I went to see a physician for a broken arm after a bike crash. During the examination, he mentioned that I had a vertebra out of place. "Can you pop it back in?" I asked. He laughingly responded, "I could, but I'm supposed to recommend surgery." I was floored. Doctors are trained to recommend *back surgery* for something as simple as a bone out of place? They fuse the spine and keep it from moving, altering your range of motion for life... something a chiropractor would just apply a little pressure to and it would resolve instantly. Really? It was at that moment that I lost all respect for the medical profession. I honor their emergency life-saving skills, but this kind of thinking is so immoral and so unconscionable, there is just no way to excuse it. I know medical doctors worked hard on their ascent, but so did Hitler. If your approach is *not* morally prioritized to (1) be minimally invasive and most economical, (2) maintain and maximize the patient's living independence, mobility, and enjoyment, and (3) seeking to cure rather than maintain sickness, then you are a Nazi in the midst of your own medical holocaust. For the rest of you, you've been lied to. When you criticize chiropractors, it stems from the propaganda you have been fed. It is time to think independently. The great victims of the sick rich and their minions at the AMA and FDA need to be reevaluated with independent judgment and proper respect.

As for patients, if you accepted back surgery and never even attempted treatment by a chiropractor because you *"heard they were quacks,"* or that *"once you go, you'll always have to go"*, you are the kind of simple-minded, gullible, and easily-controlled moron the sick rich love. Or you were lied to, and I'm sorry you accepted the lie. *Without thinking for yourself.* And you don't *always have to go*...the McKenzie Method of *self*-adjustment addresses normal spine issues brilliantly. Still, when you can't fix it yourself, what's worse: periodic $40 adjustments to counter the twists, slips, falls, and over exertions of life, or a $200,000 surgery, permanent disability, and a lifetime of being hooked on pain killers? Future patients: exercise your core. Drink more water and less wine. *Think for yourself.*

Free America from Health Care Debt

"Experts agree that our health care system is riddled with inefficiencies, excessive administrative expenses, inflated prices, poor management, and inappropriate care, waste and fraud. These problems significantly increase the cost of medical care and health insurance for employers and workers and affect the security of families."

—National Coalition on Health Care

In 2013, the United States spent 17 percent of its gross domestic product (GDP) on health care. It is projected to reach 20 percent by 2020. In contrast, health care spending accounted for 10.9 percent of the GDP in Switzerland, 10.7 percent in Germany, 9.7 percent in Canada and 9.5 percent in France, according to the Organization for Economic

Cooperation and Development. If advanced countries like our own are holding steady at 10 percent, what on Earth is causing ours to double?

"For decades, the U.S. healthcare system was the envy of the entire world. Not coincidentally, there was far less government involvement in medicine during this time. America had the finest doctors and hospitals, patients enjoyed high-quality, affordable medical care, and thousands of private charities provided health services for the poor. Doctors focused on treating patients, without the red tape and threat of lawsuits that plague the profession today. Most Americans paid cash for basic services, and had insurance only for major illnesses and accidents. This meant both doctors and patients had an incentive to keep costs down, as the patient was directly responsible for payment, rather than an HMO or government program.

The lesson is clear: when government and other third parties get involved, health care costs spiral. The answer is not a system of outright socialized medicine, but rather a system that encourages everyone – doctors, hospitals, patients, and drug companies – to keep costs down. As long as "somebody else" is paying the bill, the bill will be too high. "

—Ron Paul, M.D. and U.S. Senator

To assure the best medical care money can buy, America needs legislation passed that streamlines the industry. For one, medical insurance should be pretax to the populace. There should be caps on legal remedies regarding malpractice, so doctors can "operate" without unnecessary risk. We waste *half a trillion dollars* a year on claim paperwork and over-testing alone to minimize their liability. Astronomical lawsuits drive doctor's liability insurance premiums through the roof, and our healthcare premiums follow suit. Other countries don't permit this; we shouldn't either. One alternative is "negative outcomes" insurance proposed in House Bill HR 3076, which could be purchased by patients undergoing surgery, avoiding the immense cost and time to litigate a claim if something goes wrong.

Healthcare costs would drop drastically if the sick rich stopped trying to kill us 30 different ways. The huge amount we will save when existing cures for cancer and heart disease go mainstream will also revitalize the economy as its former victims become more active and engaged in life. "Managing disease"—like provoking war to keep the military industry profitable—will fall by the wayside as patients recognize how fraudulent omission and Pavlovian conditioning (take these pills for at least 21 days…) by pharmaceutical companies and their pushers have been used against them. Tailoring fees to the honorable and factual needs of patient and doctor is the way back to a strong healthcare system for America.

Trust Yourself: Self-Diagnosis

Once I realized that most doctors didn't have my best interests at heart, I became big into self-diagnosis and self-healing. When a professional laughs at, condemns, and ridicules me for asking questions—investing considerable energy to harass what they consider to be an immediate threat—they've discredited themselves, and I've witnessed this behavior from doctors on several occasions. Any group who uses harassing tactics is suspect, but to see it from highly educated people, now *that* is worth investigating.

We've been trained to believe that it takes 8 years to understand anything medical; that we have no right to question them, and simply must do as we are told. Better physicians have broken this trend to show that anything medical can be understood by anyone, and the majority of health issues can be acted on *independent* of a physician. Considerable experimentation can be done as well with little consequence, from preventative measures to direct disease treatment. What do you have to lose? No drugs, no large bills, no permanent medical injuries. For example, a friend of mine started having extreme, shocking pains in his side that would stop him in his tracks. Coincidentally, I began exhibiting the same symptoms. He went to the doctor first, who scheduled him for immediate kidney stone surgery at a cost of over $10,000. I found a home remedy online, and about six dollars later (a few lemons and some olive oil), was cured. My friend was prescribed medication to manage the condition indefinitely, while I made a few recommended dietary changes, and the issue didn't return. Scrutinizing your doctor is not crazy. Self-abnegation and supplication is crazy. I haven't been able to solve everything, but angina? Check. Sprains? Check. Sore throat? Congestion? Headache? Fever? Check check check.

You are capable of making most of your medical decisions and administering many of your own cures. Go online: you will find everything from age-old home remedies to the latest advances in topical applications, capsules, or recipes. Try them. Spend pennies and listen to your body before you get talked into spending hundreds or thousands. There are natural vitamins, herbs, and blends that pharmaceutical companies try and mimic to make profitable. Find the originals, pay little, and enjoy no liver-destroying side effects, no thoughts of suicide, and no addictions. Don't feed the avaricious mindset: don't help your doctor try to get rich off of every visit.

Free Farming, Free Our Food

Our food supply is monopolized by a handful of corporations with highly controversial histories. Monsanto, Syngenta, Bayer, and Dow-DuPont have bought over 200 independent seed companies and now dictate nearly everything that is planted in America. Monsanto, a chemical company rebranded as an agriculture firm, is responsible for developing some of the most toxic substances on earth: Agent Orange, Dioxin, DDT, and PCB's. They are credited with 50 toxic superfund sites where cleanup is near impossible and environmental devastation has raged on for the last fifty years. Even after Monsanto had clear evidence that the toxins were an extreme health hazard, they hid the knowledge for decades, sacrificing public safety rather than disrupt the income streams generated. Chemical companies with horrific moral atrocities on their records should not be allowed in the food industry at all; and certainly should not be permitted to control it!

I had heard Monsanto was evil for years, but never looked into it. I thought, "Fresh eyes for the usual suspects", but quickly found mass opinion to be justified. For example, Monsanto sued farmers when Monsanto's seeds would blow over into their fields and mix with the farmer's crops. Believe it or not, they sued for patent infringement! So dishonorable an approach is obvious, but right or wrong, most farmers couldn't sustain the lawsuit and their business as well. They would be forced to settle. Such farmers are morally justified to sue for GMO pollution: the contamination of their fields with unnatural agents, which fortunately, is the current trend of the law. Farmers now have legal protection against this, so the system *can* work.

Monsanto claims on their website to have launched under 150 lawsuits against American farmers over the years, wondering why, when they deal with a few hundred thousand farmers, such a small number would have given them so negative a reputation. What they don't mention are the thousands of lawsuits threatened and settled out of court *yearly* (4,500 in 2006 alone), the risk of which terrorizes their entire customer base. They employ individuals known as Seed Police, who travel the country investigating and intimidating farmers for infractions in seed storing. Farmers are encouraged to report on their neighbors, provoking such queries perhaps for competitive advantage, where accused farmers find it cheaper to pay settlements than to litigate and face Monsanto's seizure of their land and equipment. Monsanto claims that the proceeds are donated for agriculture scholarships, yet the amount taken from farmers has been as high as $68 million in a year, while the amount given charitably averages less than $1 million per year. This gives decent Americans several thousand if not millions of reasons to despise them.

In a recent folly, claiming Monsanto's product Round Up is non-toxic, GMO advocate and Monsanto lobbyist Dr. Patrick Moore said in 2015, *"You can drink a whole quart of it and it won't hurt you."* The journalist then put a glass of the weed-killer in front of him, inviting him to prove it. Refusing, he said *"I'm not stupid."* But they think we are? Glyphosate (the active ingredient in Round Up) has since been found to be carcinogenic, and 125x more toxic than regulators claimed. For all the spin and maneuvering Monsanto's representatives have done to distance themselves from past atrocities, they haven't changed.

Monsanto sues its customer base as a regular course of business, and their competitors are now following suit, leaving farmers nowhere to turn. Imagine being able to do that. That is a *coercive* monopoly, and we owe no allegiance to those who hold us under threat. It isn't easy to gain monopolizing control of a field—*fate of mankind* type of control—without deep connections. I expect that if you look into the core ownership of the firm, you will find political holding companies controlled by sheiks, kings, military generals, and ex-presidents, such as the Carlyle Group; men accustomed to control without accountability. Planning in advance for environmental lawsuits, Monsanto has layers of shell corporations they shed with each major suit, having one entity admit blame and pay penalties which amount to a small percentage of the overall profit, making it a routine cost of business. This practice should be legally disallowed, 100% *or more* of the profit relinquished, and the stench of dishonor glued to the executives and owners responsible. If the well-informed health and freedom of mankind means nothing to you, your corporation's survival means nothing to me.

Warrior Note: *Any wealthy group practicing or seeking police powers is ripe for prosecution.*

Farming regulations should be determined by a firm's range of public impact with stiff regulations for large industrial farms and light regulations for small farms. Small farms are the core of American health just as small business is the lifeblood of the American economy. The size of their operation must be considered, placing as light a burden as possible on small businesses operating on a shoestring. Seed patent laws for example have been a disaster for farmers as they have resulted in this Gestapo practice run amok. Legalizing patents for living organisms was an unsound and immoral ruling that should be overturned. Once introduced to the natural environment, seeds are out of their control, and quickly morph into something the company did not create.

By protecting the small farmer, we protect the integrity of the food supply. No one source would be in control of what is contained within the crops planted; no corrupt agenda affecting the masses could succeed. No seed monopolies or patents should be permitted: 10% of market share maximum. No conquest lawsuits that risk the existence of the small farmer should be permitted. If a considerable disparity in the size of the organizations exists (say 5 to 1 or more), all legal fees and any financial disruption that threatens the stability of the smaller should be provided up front by the larger entity that files suit.

To have the best chance to stay healthy and GMO free, buy from local farmers markets. Verify their seeds were not purchased from multinational corporations. We need biodiversity to be safe: a great variety of seeds acclimated to many different environments. Each area has its own conditions that the plants have accommodated themselves to and are best suited for. Farmers must be free to develop their own seeds, to keep them, to store them, and to replant them. This is the foundation of the farming process from its inception in America, and our health, our freedom, and ultimately our lives, depend on it.

Honest Labeling

"The very word 'secrecy' is repugnant in a free and open society. ... We decided long ago that the dangers of excessive and unwarranted concealment of pertinent facts far outweighed the dangers which are cited to justify it. "

–President John F. Kennedy

The FDA press release on genetically-modified salmon is heavy on marketing and light on facts. It states, "After an exhaustive and rigorous scientific review, FDA has arrived at the decision that AquAdvantage salmon is as safe to eat as any non-genetically engineered (GE) Atlantic salmon, and also as nutritious." This is quite a loaded sales pitch for a scientific establishment to engage in. In another thesaurus-inspired statement, "The FDA scientists rigorously evaluated extensive data submitted by the manufacturer", but the extensive raw data was not shared with the public. So how can the public know the data was not cherry-picked, or that any bad results weren't just left out? So they tell the public it was sound rather than demonstrate: "Based on sound science and a comprehensive review..." Compare this to FDA conduct on any cost-effective treatment such as EDTA for heart patients and they slow to a snail's pace. Their tone becomes riddled with doubt and obfuscation in equally non-specific language to keep it in trials indefinitely while Big Pharma attempts their own profitable versions in the marketplace (for example, there have been zero reported deaths due to Calcium Disodium EDTA in 45 years vs. Digoxin: widely used and FDA approved with NO clinical trials, yet risks a 21% increased chance of death).

The press release went on, attempting to quickly implement new labeling standards which protect special interests at the expense of consumers: *"the FDA can only require additional labeling of foods derived from GE sources if there is a material difference – such as a different nutritional profile – between the GE product and its non-GE counterpart. ...the FDA did not find any such differences."* The genetic makeup is one *glaring* difference. Our bodies often attack tampered-with cells, treating them as foreign invaders. People need to know exactly what their family is eating, but it is hard to convince an FDA spokesperson who just built a lovely addition to their home paid for by their favorite customer.

On Wall Street, the currency of favor is stock options. In pharmaceuticals, the currency of favor is patent rights. Big Pharma says to the drug approver, *"Approve this drug and we'll give you partial patent rights to it. We will then license it from you for 25% of the profit."* So getting the drug approved is a matter of when you want your new income stream to start. CDC Advisor Dr. Paul Offit, who received $29 million (minimum) for a vaccine he helped create a market for, exclaimed *"It's like winning the lottery!"* Of course, the gamble taken is with our children's lives. This is part of the revolving door: industry executives may work at the USDA today, but they could work at Monsanto or the FDA tomorrow. On a special project, they may complete the proposal and oversee development at the private company or university, then "quit", moving their office to the FDA in the next phase to walk it through the approval process, then move to the USDA for implementation and legal protection to ensure its profitability. There is no objectivity and no independent studies, just horrendous conflicts of interest, lots of creative fraud, and no regulations requiring otherwise.

Nothing shouts *"The FDA is corrupt"* louder than the drug commercials we see on TV these days. The first half of the ad is of beautiful people sailing, or laughing over drinks with friends, or a couple holding hands at sunset.

The second half of the ad is *"If you are bleeding out of your eyes, if your heart eats a hole through your chest or if you start randomly killing people, Euthanoxin might not be right for you."* Common sense adds *"If this drug requires a thousand disclaimers, the FDA should never have released it, but our partners want profits sooner than later, and we want our kickbacks."* At $100 million for a clinical drug trial, it is easy for a big company to get an unproven experimental drug released for sale. It is almost impossible to get FDA approval for a proven treatment that helps the people but offers little profit, and may pose a threat to products of a large company. Return on investment is their primary focus; the good of the patient isn't even on their radar. This should tell you that these large organizations are not trustworthy and that your health relies on your independence from them.

Monsanto's website states, "The American Medical Association (AMA) supports FDA's approach and approved a formal statement asserting that there is no scientific justification for special labeling of foods containing GM ingredients." So the AMA, the most morally discredited organization in medicine, agrees that honesty and full disclosure are not scientific requirements? Who is surprised?

Monsanto's website continues, "We oppose current initiatives to mandate labeling of ingredients developed from GM seeds in the absence of any demonstrated risks." Well, as a free-thinking American, I oppose NOT labeling ingredients made from GM seeds in the absence of convincing proof that they are safe: short-term, long-term, for all ages and physical conditions that may encounter the product. They go on to say, "It could be interpreted as a warning or imply that food products containing these ingredients are somehow inferior to their conventional or organic counterparts." That is the universal grafter's wish: to avoid disclosing that their shiny, "high quality" products are actually Chinese junk. Besides, Monsanto and the Franken-fish enterprise shot themselves in the foot already: telling the public you have done research that shows your products are safe without sharing the research carries the same stigma as outright lying, and passing off responsibility for your product's safety to a government office or the market itself is even less excusable.

If we continue to permit this axis of evil to rotate, eventually food labels will carry the kind of extensive disclaimers pharmaceuticals do. But such companies are pursuing a way around that as well. Preparing for disaster, Monsanto has simply written self-serving legislation and lobbied for it in every corrupt nook and cranny of Washington. The Monsanto Protection Act grants them legal immunity from the lawsuits that will come when GMO's are ultimately found to be carcinogenic. Even if they sicken or kill everyone, they want to keep the money and foist damage and recovery costs onto the American taxpayers, just as the vaccine manufacturers did with their Act.

Ultimately, as long as labels are honest, it is your choice to buy clean, pure, natural foods, or cheap, synthetic garbage that looks like food, but leaves you hollow and kills you slowly. If I see "Distributed By…" instead of "Made In…" I drop it immediately, aware that they are trying to hide the controversy surrounding its origin. I buy "Free Range…" and "Organic" when I see it. The only reason to fight clear and complete labeling is that corrupt companies are left with the risk of lying about ingredients and processes, and the fraud suits and public relations disasters that follow. If political subversion wins and we are simply not allowed to know, we can do nothing about it except NOT BUY (and a boycott would bring them to their knees). Think of the food allergies kids have today, the careful diets their parents prepare, and that they would be forced to play Russian roulette with their children's health instead. This is unconscionable. Who comes first? America's kids, or monopolies imposing products that nobody wants anyway? Only buy from companies who are 100% transparent with clear, complete, and honest labeling: what the ingredients are, what the packaging is made of *and coated with,* how products are grown, the living conditions of livestock, etc. If they don't share this information willingly, assume the worst. Make sure the companies you do business with offer public inspection tours of their facilities as well to prove their claims, and open their lab books to scrutiny. If they say *"It's the government's job to make sure our product is safe, not ours"*, dump them immediately.

Lovely, free, inquiring, scrutinizing Americans deserve to know exactly what they are buying at all times. We have to know if a product is artificial and what kind of motives developed it. Domination of the food supply is a perfect biochemical weapon delivery system. With companies who have disregarded public safety so blatantly in the past, there is always the possibility they have baked in some latent gene designed to kill us all (or will at some point), so I for one, would rather eat organic. Spirit Murdering psychosis aside, a large segment of the population believes that genetic modification is the wrong direction for science to be headed in, and the last people they are going to trust are military/industrial chemical companies with extensive histories of developing toxic substances, polluting the world with them, and lying about it. The same goes for any of their like-minded competitors, subsidiaries, associates, suppliers, and past, present, or future owners. Just stay on your side of the planet.

No GMO products should be released for public consumption until long-term *independent* studies have been done to verify they are non-toxic and to identify any long-term consequences. I for one do not want to eat anything genetically modified, especially when modified by frauds, and I certainly don't want to be tricked into eating it. No unchecked company self-certifications should be permitted regarding issues of public safety. No patents for living organisms. The cost and structure of clinical trials should be reformed to accommodate our sacred American pioneers: individual doctors and scientists from whom truly revolutionary ideas originate. Any group with a large market share, especially those brazen enough to assume police powers, must have public oversight and be held accountable for their actions; not handed passes for misconduct or potential risks to the populace. The People are more important than any depraved revolving door scheme. It is up to us to *re*form a more perfect union.

Free the Atmosphere

"Mistakes of this size are never made innocently."
-Ayn Rand

Nowadays, we see jets fly high overhead leaving long contrails; but instead of dissipating quickly as normal, the contrails expand wider and wider until they become a general haze. As described by Professor David Keith on the BBC show HARDTalk, jet-sprayed aerosols, known as chemtrails, are the government's attempt to control climate change. But what is in this haze?

Environmentalists and concerned citizens around the world have been monitoring a buildup of heavy metals in air, rainwater, and soil in areas of heavy chemtrail activity. Soil samples in Alberta show aluminum 7 times higher than safe limits. A 2008 air quality report in Phoenix showed barium at 278x toxic limits, copper at 98x toxic limits, manganese at 5,820x toxic limits, zinc at 593x toxic limits, cadmium at 126x toxic limits, chromium at 282x toxic limits, nickel at 169x toxic limits, aluminum at 6,400x toxic limits, iron at 28,000x toxic limits, magnesium at 5x toxic limits, potassium at 793x toxic limits, and sodium at 16x toxic limits. Forty more samples have been tested since then, most showing high levels of aluminum. Several websites and organizations are now collecting reports on elevated toxin levels from around the world in soil, air, water, and blood samples.

Should a group wish to choke off all life on the planet, this seems like a good way to do it. The Nazi's deceived people to their deaths by herding them into a box and gassing them. We spray hornet's nests and spiders to keep them at bay, and now we are being sprayed like bugs. The cover story is geoengineering to help the environment or weather modification for military purposes, but the results are poisons, well above safety limits, raining down on all plant, animal, and human life, polluting the entire food chain. In these areas, plants are dying, wildfires are raging, and nothing will grow. More recent reports involve the jet-aerosol spraying of lithium and freeze-dried blood over cities. Lithium is highly toxic and is prescribed by psychiatrists as a mood stabilizer. Why not Prozac? Or maybe eggs and toast? Breakfast anytime: just step outside.

We experience yearly cycles—spring, summer, fall, and winter—but there are 1000 year cycles, 10,000 year cycles, and more. Some Earth cycles are so big we cannot yet comprehend their sources. They could have multiple causative factors working in conjunction to yield specific conditions, none of which we can control. What can we control? Limiting pollution is inherently sound; there is direct evidence that all living things benefit. Get close to an exhaust pipe and you start coughing; easy enough to validate. So generating pollution on an industrial scale, such as spraying megatons of noxious chemicals and nano-metals into the atmosphere that are detrimental to all life, is *not* rational. To ascribe some loopy scientific justification for it just defies belief over what is not addressed.

At a climate geoengineering conference in 2009, solar expert Dane Wigington questioned, "Numerous air quality studies including from the California Air Quality Resource Board have named sub-micron sized particulates as being particularly harmful for human respiration. Through all the discussions today, I have not heard any mention of this fallout and has this been studied? And also the effects of a highly reactive metal like aluminum on toxifying soils and waters?" Professor David Keith responded, "...it's not even close to being an issue." Mr. Wigington replied, "So ten megatons of aluminum dumped into the atmosphere would have no human health impacts?" Professor Keith responded, "We haven't done anything serious on alumina and so there could be something terrible we find tomorrow; we haven't looked at it." Professor Keith maintained that this was all theoretical and had not progressed beyond mathematical calculations, but evidence suggests they have been spraying such aerosols since the 1990's. Government agencies are dumping these compounds in the sky around the world but claim they have performed NO studies to see if it may be harmful to human and animal life, plant life, and crops, and that they may have a big problem down the road...they simply don't know. They have no idea if aluminum is harmful to Man? Barium? Strontium? This is not blissful ignorance; this is science fraud and attempted mass murder. Toxic heavy metals are bad for people; in nano form, they are devastating. Saving the atmosphere requires human poisons? I don't think so. Getting rid of humans requires human poisons.

The cover story isn't even sound. Professor Keith claims the haze hides the earth from the sun, helping it to cool, when like sitting in a hot car with the windows rolled up, it does the exact opposite. Climate scientist Joyce Penner explained that thin clouds such as those produced by the jet-sprayed aerosols will warm the atmosphere (accelerating the effects of global warming), a viewpoint backed by data and the government's own reports. It should be noted that Professor Keith's work extends beyond applied physics, as he also serves as Professor of *Public Policy*. It is not surprising a media spokesman has been assigned to reinterpret this homicidal program for public consumption.

What we breathe, eat, and drink needs to be clean. All safety norms for toxins we encounter need to be front and center and monitored openly and carefully. If anything is out of line, it is our constitutional right (those reserved by the people) to stop what is being done—by tax revolt or other government boycott—until the imbalance is corrected. Our founding fathers inserted such a statement to address what they could not anticipate. We should add an amendment to the Constitution to ban the dumping of toxins by any organized group in our air, water, or land.

Living Business: The Abstract Life of an Organization

Not all enterprises are evil: in fact, most are not, as Self-made Man forms organizations, too. Many moral lessons can be learned by studying America's finest corporations. They are the perfect example of men uniting in order to produce bounty—a fair, deserved, profitable result. Profit means that after a day's effort, you have something to show for it. Profitability is a sign of living competence, not of greed. A business has an abstract life like a person, and profit is its lifeblood. Even in the process of learning, to end up with a greater sum is to profit intellectually. We see that plants and animals run a process like our own, accumulating, processing, and storing food for the sustenance of *their* lives. As wealth and profit are fundamental patterns of life for *all* organisms, those critical of it are simply damning us for our ability to live.

We hear that money is the root of all evil, but money is simply a tool that allows products to pass easily between producers and consumers. It is easier to trade with a standard medium than having to hope a vacuum cleaner salesman has use for your stair-master. No, there is nothing wrong with the medium of money; nothing wrong with the honest, peaceful accumulation of capital, and nothing wrong with producing more than you consume, as profit permits innovation. These are *essential* life-serving, forward-thinking, sound, civil, and moral principles. With full understanding and respect for the effort we all put forth to create products that make life easier for everyone, I for one, salute you.

Sound Hierarchy

The man of greatest capacity at every level within the organization should lead. He should be chosen by his people, and replaced when he is no longer effective (if the life of the organization is to come first). A business has a dynamic just like a human body, which gets sick if its focus strays or if it comes to require a specialty which is different from that of its head. As a part of the company's body, each employee contributes to or detracts from its health with every action they take in its name.

The products of men will have the integrity of those who built them. Those who earn a fortune by moral means in a free system of exchange have accumulated a wealth of trust, and it is a rational measure of pride, but be careful not to go overboard. I have often witnessed a company executive looking for a way to persuade his people to stand behind the company's proud, long-range goals as if they were their own; to display pure loyalty to his dream as if it was their own. If your campaign doesn't come with stock options, forget it. Such a mindset only comes with ownership. Mass support for another individual or his corporation above and beyond their own lives isn't sound—it isn't moral and it isn't ideal. All individuals work for their own health and objectives within the corporation—job satisfaction, advancement and financial reward—and they should. The company's health is a result of managing these forces wisely—having all of the independent entities flying in formation while they are on your time.

The Pride of Competition

When businesses try to steal customers from each other, it isn't actually stealing; there is no moral violation. No one has a right to patronage; all market activity is voluntary. If men dislike a product or if it is too complex they won't buy it and will find another way to satisfy their needs. Our most complex products, such as computers, will never extend beyond the range of an individual's comprehension for effective use; the free market will never allow such a breach. It is in every businessman's best interest that his products stay within the conceptual range and efficiency of the user and that he continually seeks to improve their attractiveness to that end.

The battles between *real* Self-made Men are civil, honest, and fair. The spoils go to whoever does it best, and whoever doesn't, often ends up working for whoever does. To lose a corporate battle is not a life or death issue, it is a spiritual issue, and a challenge to come back better, stronger, and prouder than before, often catching the leader off-guard. It is a genuine pursuit, and it's fun! With a free economy, there is room for many levels of talent and of product quality—take cars for instance. We buy economy until we can afford luxury, with many different brands and styles to choose from. By competing in a vast marketplace, many entrepreneurs get to see how well they perform in the role of leader, and their ability determines their position among the great firms of the world.

Competition spurs discovery, and results in the more efficient use of human energy. An advance of technology is an advance in wealth for all—regardless of how jobs are restructured for the change. The freer a field is, the better it is for everyone. Fierce competition, as in the computer industry, just results in more stars, greater talent, more numerous fortunes, and a purer distribution of wealth than has ever existed. It is said that Microsoft has more millionaire *secretaries* than any other firm.

Healthy Morale

Morale is the most underrated, avoided, and seemingly incomprehensible issue in business. Bad morale has a silently devastating undercurrent; it is cancer to a business. Why is the subject avoided? Because it involves the mystical, uncertain realm of morality. Like it or not, managers are responsible for a happy staff. As a body is only as healthy as its cells, its cells must be healthy, and people are the cells of a business. Much more than protoplasm, people harness the capacity of volition, but as an analogy, people, like cells, have a specific nature which must be accounted for.

An employer/employee relationship is governed by and must contain all of the essential attributes of any human relationship: rationality, civility, honesty, mutual interest, and mutual benefit. Good managers don't require submission in a world where force is banned; that is a psychological remnant of the past. If you deserve your position as a leader, you are beyond tantrums, beyond neurotic dominance, and you are able to treat everyone in your organization with deference. Likewise, responsible employees are objective, sincere and perform tasks as or better than expected. They are emotionally mature and apply themselves as their interview promised they would. Satisfied employees and employers get the job done together, and look to accommodate and foster the deepest goals of both. We all have dreams.

Morale is defined as the general mood of employees determined by the working conditions provided by management. Respect for one's superiors does not come from enforcing inessential issues such as strict start and stop times. It cannot be had by steering people at every step. Instead, decent morale comes from communicating what is crucial to accomplish, providing the tools, and leaving employees free to achieve. All minds approach their work in patterns tailored to their own psychological makeup, and they must be free to function unimpeded. A good manager lets them address tasks by their unique means. With a successful performance, everyone deserves acknowledgement. To be valued is much more than spiritual gratification; it assures our living security. As most people live check to check, that comfort has very real psychological consequences. My own custom when reviewing a performance issue with an employee is to project why the improvements or new skills are needed for their role in future projects. Try this yourself and witness the sighs of relief you hear. You will likely see a renewed invigoration and increased sense of loyalty from them as well.

The Cancer of Corporate Dysfunction

While a free system of exchange is what we should honor and preserve, history has recorded countless abuses inflicted when the Fear-driven gain control. All men in positions of authority work to actualize their own psychological bias towards life or death. As I've said in trying consultations, *"We can work to advance your business, or I can help you run it into the ground – whatever the hell you want to do."* As employees, we are just limbs. Such an arm can be alive and well, just wiggling away, while the rest of the company is on its deathbed. If the head is faulty, it will die, and it should die.

It never ceases to amaze me that the biggest contributor to a profit and loss statement—human resources—has nothing to do with profit and loss. Company presidents leave it in the hands of some amiable ink-blot specialist, restricts the hiring budget, and closes his door to the issue of manpower. Employees are then hired by the "low pay and high hopes" method. Quality is driven out while schooled incompetence and fresh inexperience is then allowed to destroy the company.

Many companies hire by degree, saving themselves the trauma of personal evaluation. But degrees don't make money. How will a business fail if MBA is after the president's name? Will it spiral to the left instead of the right? Smart managers assemble teams of the best available, whose selection is based on ability. To attract it, you must be able to identify it. To keep it, you must have the deepest regard for it.

Irrational Employers

Bad managers tailor their management style to their own cowardice, seeking the protective exoskeleton of a company's structure to unwittingly obey. Fear impairs his ability to distinguish essential profitable actions from inessentials, so company policy and supplication replace his judgment. They bow above and backstab below, undermining those abler and training their subordinates to do likewise. Corporate dysfunction reveals the same elements found in Communism—the manic pursuit of the sure thing—which is what all Fear-driven men do when they are in control. Its people become dysfunctional due to low morale and misguided objectives, and no one can figure out why. The problem persists because often, upper managers were products of the "low pay and high hopes" formula as well.

Bad managers expect supplication—the King and Queen syndrome of old. They expect to be bowed to and to command the whip-driven slave worker who is not to be relied on to think. With no internal frame of moral reference, the fear-based mind panics and operates by the latest business fad. When spooked, he breaks that direction and goes off in another, leaving everyone lost without clear expectations. Employees must respond to his constantly shifting center of gravity.

He crawls before his customers, submitting to their will, rational or not. He rapes his suppliers, violating agreements and bullying, resulting in lower quality and stronger competitors. To him, no violation of ethics is out of the question—lying, pressuring, even annoying his customers to gain a sale, with deception, telemarketing, and personal invasion. He lobbies for unfair advantages and exploits international slave labor, to bar others from reaching markets he wishes to hold captive. This is predation instead of creation—using others up instead of respecting the universal pattern of life in turn.

If you are a manager, ask yourself: how many people did my company throw out of work in the last recession? Is my business now geared to shed employees fast, or to properly weather downturns without disrupting lives? Is there any reason to expect loyalty as a result?

Irrational Employees

Employees are equally prone to functioning from fear. The submissive employee acts like a captive, relishing any excuse to despise those above him. He seeks an exoskeletal frame as well, such as strict adherence to company policy, rank, or seniority, as substitute for his productive value to the company. He lies, steals, cheats time, and takes credit for the work of others, and when hostilities arise, he is defeated in advance, acting like a child being dragged away for a spanking.

Ultimately, rational employers pay for ability, so there is no need for employees to feel they hold a weaker position. We need each other. It doesn't matter if employees are replaceable; employers are, too.

Marxist Labor Unions

There are good unions and there are bad unions. I have seen both first hand, and the difference will make or break a company. In watching Japanese union workers, I was impressed by the focus of their performance. There is a cultural aspect involved that demands pride in their work. To do a bad job would bring shame; a mortal blow. In America, we have a culture of freedom, but many abuse it by claiming it means *"the right to have no discipline."* This is how we get beaten.

Here is what it is like to be hired into a union of socialist design: Instead of joining a plan for the greater good, suddenly you are lost among the undifferentiated—among the mean and small—and are then penalized for displaying anything more. You find out that the company is your enemy—that everything you thought made a good employee is now bad—that the lowest around you is now your equal, and your burden. They acknowledge seniority, not performance, disallowing effort to outpace lethargy. Their mass bares its teeth when exposed to any hint of personal accountability. Despite the thinly veiled, murderous smiles welcoming you, you can barely hide from yourself the fact that you have joined a hate group. It is the deeper brotherhood of all human beings that has been betrayed here. Unions may have begun as protection for unfairly treated workers, but with a Marxist ideology, they become a collection of *us against them* Spirit Murderers: malicious guardians of the Submission/ Domination Axis, and that's all.

Marxist unions damn automation, yet propose no means to remain competitive. You rarely hear any ideas for improving efficiency; you never hear them addressing the company's competitiveness or considering any sane reason why human beings are in business. Instead we hear their nineteenth-century reproaches against working conditions. For example, during our country's intellectually-degraded pro-communist period, American railways were bullied into focusing on the livelihood of their workers, not on moving freight. The purpose had been lost—that of utilizing every bit of a business's potential in the profitable pursuit of life as an abstract ideal—not the sheer naked survival of workers, and it virtually destroyed the industry.

Now, it is *certainly* the duty of company leaders to assure there will be work for those they hire. People depend on their income's continuance, and count on those above to keep it growing or at least stable. But when managers strip the company of its wealth instead, leaving it unprepared for a downturn, causing mass layoffs and hardship, the employees have a right to band together and fight. This is where a proper union weighs in to protect workers. In today's climate, we have huge hundred-year old businesses that are no longer run by their founders, but by principals having no vested interest in them. Such executives serve on each other's boards, voting for mutual overcompensation, amounting to little more than embezzlement, and when things go south, they jump ship with golden parachutes. We must make it harder for corrupt individuals and their networks to destroy companies from the top, with jail terms and recovery of the stolen capital, which caused the business to falter. Still, no business exists solely for its workers. Workers exist in their context for the product alone. Losing a job is not the equivalent of losing one's life, and there is no such thing as *the right to a job*. When a business is mismanaged or the country goes into recession, restoration of economic calm is found after a shakeout, which rids the waste of oversupply, and redistributes workers among the fields were they are actually needed.

The truth is a Marxist union brings—not craftsmen or manufacturing expertise to an industry—but *violence,* as it is a power organized *specifically* for the disruption of the enterprise. Such a union's morale is dogmatically intended to *maintain* an all-time low. They are convinced that at work they deserve to sleep, to be drunk, to skip three days a week, and be totally unaccountable for their task, then to proclaim their inestimable worth and strike over compensation. That such people can live with so shameful a disregard for virtue is an abomination—almost as bad as its tolerance. A new employee with good intentions, trying to use sound administrative and moral judgment will find his efforts trounced by the very evil the system is designed to protect. He will be forced into cover-ups, strikes, walk-outs and a host of other immature or hostile activities, shamefully conspiring against goodwill, where adults embarrass themselves in a psychological predicament children should never have to see.

In an age of immense corporate graft, unions have been one of the few organizations to come forward and protect the people. If they want to survive long-term, they must break any tie to Karl Marx and his hostile propaganda. Unions need to acquire a sound operating philosophy and develop a "backbone of the nation" kind of culture we can all be proud of. They must become master craftsman once more, and restore the pride and confidence we feel when seeing MADE IN THE USA on a product. Otherwise, the only recompense Self-made businessmen have against poor conduct is the one line union membership is designed to prevent: *"You're fired!"*

Clean Government

"It is the duty of the patriot to protect his country from its government." —Thomas Paine

What do we want from our government? First of all, a safe, secure environment; a sound base from which we can build and grow. We imagine an army that runs to our defense and noble individuals dealing with foreign officials to protect us and guarantee fairness between nations. But often, we straddle the dilemma of assuring government effectiveness versus suffering government interference. The expected result is peace and stability; our pleasant contemplation of never-ending tomorrows, enjoying today and looking forward to every step we take along the path of our lives. Here are some key areas that our freedom and stability depend on.

The Separation of Church and State

Every business ethic is based on an experienced understanding of long term cause and effect; of an inherent respect for right and wrong, driven by a *logical* standard, which often conflicts with and requires defiance of, religious instruction. Our laws reflect this dilemma as well.

From birth, we have associated our own goodness to our religious ties, never thinking to comprehend the possibility of another source—our own life-generating power. Throughout history, we have been told that the purpose of morality was "to serve God." War-torn European citizens needed relief from this view, which from one dominion to another, kept men at odds. They came to the New World to establish a civilization that dispensed with ideological struggle, based solely on the common respect of what is *physically* necessary for all men to survive in peace. The actual focus of morality *in practice,* is and always has been, to preserve and further human life. A proper definition of morality leaves no foothold on the human body, and *that* is why it has been kept from us for so long.

By spotlighting indigence instead of fostering ability, by giving preference to faith versus rationality, by supporting social adjustment rather than independence, by advising mercy towards guilt instead of justice for innocence, organized religion *inverted* morality and turned it against Man. Instead of a pat on the back for our effort, we were infused with an answerless guilt. This moral inversion has allowed us no connection between healthy spirituality and the work we have done. We have never received the spiritual reward we deserve, by proper moral acknowledgement of our greatest productive endeavor—American free enterprise, and that fact reinforces the case for our separation of church and State.

Capitalism

The birth of our country was the birth of an idea of how men were to engage each other—for once having the courage not to cannibalize. No two philosophies are more desperately needed or are more intentionally subverted than morality and economics (and the subversion of the first makes the subversion of the second possible). A proper code of ethics focuses on the entity it protects: the individual. Sound economics focuses on the proper interrelation of individuals (not sociology, democracy, Communism, or any governmental body, as is often taught). Capitalism simply stands for the right of an individual citizen to make his own economic decisions—to use his own judgment in deciding what to offer, what to buy, and who to trade with. Any other system denies him these rights (and the use of cognition), tells him what he needs, and forces him to accept it.

Why Socialism could gain acceptance by totally violating the natural requirements of the entity it governed isn't unfathomable anymore, but it is certainly unforgivable. Self-made man would say, "Under capitalism, I can work as hard as I want and keep the results? Awesome!" While Fear-driven man would say, "Under socialism, whether I work or not, I get a cut of what others make? Awesome!" Capitalism rewards the best foot anyone puts forward. Socialism declares that society as a whole should own everything to assure equalitarian distribution, without addressing the equality of effort. They attempt to sustain the unproductive by harnessing the productive, but the good of others, or the "public good," can never violate the good of an individual. The individual *is* the measure. Look at Marxist dogma and you won't see any complex or carefully deliberated laws, but only threats and reproaches—the result of an uneducated and undisciplined consciousness looking to defy itself. At this time in history, you will see socialists decrying the failure of capitalism as a confirmation of their own agenda, but it is not capitalism that has failed. Capitalism in its purest form is called laissez-faire, meaning unregulated free-enterprise. But morally speaking, "without government regulation" does not mean *without* standards. Industries are expected to *self*-regulate and guarantee quality in graduated levels. High standards were thought to be the natural result of competition, but with a heavily-indebted populace, the cheapest product that promises more than it can deliver wins, bringing us right back to "slick-salesman and sucker" cannibalism. Capitalism is a sound institutional structure and has not failed us. *Fraud* on an enormous scale is what failed us;

fraud in the financial markets and a mutated business culture of executive embezzlement—men who strip the lifeblood out of companies in defiance of their proper operation. These men are NOT the Self-made, and deserve no moral protection in his name. They are world-robbing pirates deserving time and restitution.

That you can find a job that matches your own interests, that both you and your employer have a choice in the matter of arrangements and that you work steadily to receive a regular paycheck, the world has a political label for you: Capitalist, and a corresponding hate group. But in fact, capitalism is the only socioeconomic system that completes the pattern of life, respecting Man's nature and securing the land for his *potential* stature. It leaves him free to choose his own loyalties, free to test his adult capacities, and to do it all *alone*, without the fear of being devoured. To answer the age-old question fought over since the Cold War, "Who is going to build a better world?" That's right, the builders.

Responsible Politicians

The affairs of a country are not unlike the affairs of a major corporation, and of course the most important issue of peacetime prosperity is *solvency* and sound financial management. We need politicians who can comprehend that the essentials of one life apply to one thousand, and to one billion. Those we select win our confidence by showing they understand and can work with an integrated view of existence—how social interaction can only follow free individual action, and that our institutions must respect the sound fundamentals of both. A friend of the people does not provide men with freebies at any level. He frees them from the slavery of providing those freebies to other men.

Many Presidents have become historic names, while others are all but forgotten. George Washington was historic even while he lived; there has never been another President like him. Lincoln's calm honor and intelligence shined through the catastrophic realities of the Civil War, while Franklin D. Roosevelt's memory survives mainly due to the trauma surrounding his period—the Great Depression and World War II. John F. Kennedy stood for all that a sound, loyal American *should* stand for—he was another Lincoln, while Johnson fed our people into the furnace, starting with his own predecessor. Then there is Andrew Jackson—my favorite President—the man who killed the private banking monopoly and paid off the national debt, both which *must* be done again. He flaunted the power of the Presidency as a true grass roots American, supporting tariffs and dodging bullets; my kind of guy. He knew exactly what he was doing as chief executive, exactly who the greatest threat to our freedom was, and he wasn't afraid to face it, and that is just the kind of leader we need today.

A man fit for office has seen enough of the world to encompass an experienced view, so he is at least in his thirties. He has a solid legal, business, and military background so that he is wise, realistic, profit and freedom oriented, and is conservatively attuned not to risk it. He is fully accountable, honestly using State funds for State obligations. He is passionate about America, respects the Republic, respects American sovereignty, our moral standing, and our leadership example among nations. He understands the truth of banking history and sound economics and watches the country's checkbook *closely*. He has seen it all, and he is no patsy. He knows when he is being lied to. He knows who is pulling whose strings, and he is not about to spend his life as a puppet or a fool for evil. He is not a master liar, but a master of reason. His job is to uphold the Constitution—an obligation by moral choice—and regardless of his party affiliation, his protection of the strong, independent, stable, and healthy living flow of the people is his highest awareness and responsibility.

Regardless of whether he ever attains the presidency, a responsible politician shows his respect for the Republic by never undermining due process. He knows his role as Congressman or Senator is critical to the Republic; that there is a balance of power to guarantee public representation, and his fully coherent dedication is necessary to assure that the conscious deliberation of issues and others are checked. He knows how cowards use power, and he isn't one of them.

Political priorities in brief are first and foremost, *order*—to secure the internal and external safety of the citizens. Second is the financial health and credit of the government, which assures the longevity and independent grasp of its power structure. Third is political sovereignty, or purity from foreign or corrupt influences detrimental to national security, prosperity, and political integrity. Since the Federal Reserve Act was passed in 1913, we have had only one stable leg on the floor.

No private interest should be granted a power which threatens the prevailing order. The conviction of our Forefathers should never be lost, and should remain at the base of any legislation proposed. *"Man's motive power is his moral code."* -Atlas Shrugged. It was our Founding Father's dedication to moral values that made our society possible—a system designed to protect the human spirit, which has manifested itself as skyscrapers, spacecraft and long, peaceful, happy lives. I have never encountered a more honorable group of leaders, nor a better fundamental system of economics; certainly no politician today attempting to alter the system can compete. It is crucial that the founding principles of our country be preserved in their morally sound, original form.

BENJAMIN FRANKLIN

Franklin was a man who respected existence and consciousness, verbatim. He knew that existence itself required him to practice specific processes in order to advance, and he held it in his best interest to support a country that respected this requirement. In many other countries at the time and even today, rational cognition was considered treason, but his thoughtful innocence as a holder of public trust stuns me even now. He made every piece of reasoning complete in itself, bringing deliberation to an art form, and showed how any man, no matter how modest of intellect, can grasp and follow the moral path when those of strength have the honor to present it. With so straight-forward, calm, and thoughtful an approach, he stands as a monument to what is meant when we think of an American.

Many politicians were shocked that Benjamin Franklin did not tuck public money away from the war effort into his own private accounts as so many other generals did. It wasn't that Franklin put the country's interest ahead of his own; Franklin knew that an act of cowardice was not in his own best interest. He knew that the fate of a Republic that secured his freedom was his highest self-interest, and that becoming a petty thief was not. Having brought so many ideas in politics, science, and societal flow that are still in use, his use of moral energy was phenomenal—and timeless. In salute to him, his soldiers often drew their swords; a display that enraged inferior generals. That so purely moral a man has ever walked the Earth surely means a trail exists for the rest to pick up on.

The Constitution

Just as science looks at subatomic particles where existence cannot be subdivided further, our Constitution respects the requirements of each individual life. Our Constitution bans force in all its forms. It decentralizes power and spreads it around—granting sovereignty to all men, seeing his mind and path as endlessly unique and clearing the way for that potential. It steps beyond the

Submission/Domination Axis into what interaction *should be* among men, and holds them to it. It dissolves all class wars, as anyone can reach any level they are willing to strive for. It empowers everyone to manage their own affairs—showing belief in the people, not just in a leader—and puts in place rules to restrain the government so that the people are never at the mercy of one man's promise. Our Constitution fixes what can rationally be fixed, and leaves fluid what must remain so. Due to this, for 300 years, men have had a stable environment in which to thrive.

Human energy is only safe where predation is disallowed by law. Only in America and other environments similar in design can there be great free enterprises, allowing a man's energy to be open to the world and spread across a continent. It is only in the realm of legislation where predation is disconnected from sensate awareness and losses are sustained with no awareness of a danger—where specific victims are chosen without their knowledge or consent. Self-made man has gathered all the key variants of evil in social action, compiled throughout history to provide basic legal protection for every man's benefit, called the Bill of Rights. It is such a document that states *explicitly* that the purpose of a government is to protect its people, an end to which all other intentions must yield.

The great rights of mankind must *expressly* be declared, whose honor must supersede all other governmental action or statutes if they are deemed by this standard unconstitutional. Its purpose in practice is to *qualify* power, to guard against legislative and executive abuses and protect would be prey against its predator. In all social realms, every man must be free to think, speak, and disseminate their ideas to those interested, by their own means. To do so, no peaceable gathering may be disallowed (or herded into *free speech zones*)—which is often a tactic to quell mass dissention. No governmental stand may be taken for a particular religion, religious persecution being the reason our settlers left England to begin with. As individuals can encounter others with violent intentions and officers cannot accompany every citizen, we retain the right to bear arms. This doesn't keep people safe from tyranny as any third world country is evidence of; it is a street self-defense issue, but it certainly makes domination over the populace more difficult, and gives the people a chance if they decide enough is enough. We are protected from unreasonable search and seizure as probable cause must exist, with a warrant stating the specific illegalities sought. The confiscation of our property for public use without just compensation is disallowed. The Constitution forbids depravation of life, liberty, or property without due process of law. If we are accused of a crime, it guarantees us a speedy public trial by jury, for us to be informed of the accusation, and to be confronted by our accusers. It provides protection for the witnesses and provides us with legal counsel. We are granted jury trials in civil cases as well. Excessive bail, fines, and cruel and unusual punishments so well developed in the Middle Ages are all forbidden. These are all elements throughout history that men have suffered at the hands of Spirit

Murderers, and with America as proof, men flourish without.

The Bush administration overrode the Constitution and brought all the evils of illegitimate government back with the Patriot Act, which was anything but patriotic. This legislation must be abolished and its outgrowths dismantled if we are to be free, safe, and secure into the future.

The overall sum of how Americans feel about their country can be seen in the elements of pride that citizens of any country would like to feel: 1) That our freedom of action is protected. 2) That respect is shown for our ability to think and remain sovereign. 3) The fairness with which our government treats all people, foreign and domestic. 4) The responsible use of force inside and outside of our country, guided by logical laws and forthright international agreements. 5) The protection our system provides, instead of the peril it could cause. 6) As a nation is just a large group of families, that our system fosters our best—in individuals and children—and doesn't look to rob us of our freedoms. 7) That sound, mature, accountable men are in control, and are rewarded by the people for their integrity. To a great extent, this is what we have in America, which is a constant barometer of our civil virtues.

Still, it is a delusion, even as a patriot, to believe that Americans are a special race of men, somehow better than those on other continents. If there were no savage men here—eager to exploit and butcher others to take what they are incapable of securing by honorable means—such explicit protections would not be necessary. To combat this evil within, the Self-made Fathers of America made sure the Constitutional provisions were straight-forward and enforceable by the courts. It is further stated that the rights listed in the Constitution do not deny others retained by the people; in other words, *the people come first.* The rights of the individual must supersede the rights of any groups of men. A mind must always be free to determine its own course. It must be free to disengage the approach of others and dissent. As such, all men, regardless of social standing, race, origin, religion, sex, or age are guaranteed equal protection under the law. They may be punished *only* for legally defined offenses and taxed *only* by popular consent.

The government is not our master. It is our tool, to be used and defined as we see fit, evidenced by the nature of our Constitution. Our representatives in Congress should be the guardians of our fundamental premises. Their good or evil can be gauged by their legislative leanings relative to the Constitution's initial intent.

Essential Services

Society is an abstract concept, defining that state of interaction we face while moving from our homes to our work and back. Proper civics secure this flow for all men. We have electricity and plumbing for human convenience, and government is for the same purpose. We don't live for *its* sake. Our stability comes from our social mediums being held constant—sound roads, sound laws, and a stable money supply, securing unrestricted commerce between those in a policeable province. Our police force protects us from harm and protects the property we have made or acquired. Our armed forces do the same by protecting us from outside threats, be they invasions (planned disasters), or natural disasters. Our city planning and road commissions ensure an efficient flow between work and home, (and *of* work and home, given our water/sewer and utility services). Our pleasure travel became possible only by establishing what we needed to live: trade routes. Civilization's priority is ensuring the flow itself, so roads come before houses (not meaning their existence, but their location). Our executive branch of government determines the use of our armed forces (checked by congress) and all foreign relations, hostile or peaceful. Our legislative branch determines our policies towards other nations, as well as outlining proper legal relations between citizens.

Our societal organization provides for every likely mishap, so that we needn't feel guilty in not stopping beside every broken down car. With a clearly defined hierarchy of life—its interruption being the foremost issue to avoid—outside of a life or death situation, the stranded motorist gets a call to those paid for this purpose: rescue vehicles, tow trucks or whatever is appropriate. What is most important to the citizens is *order:* that no form of anarchy be allowed to reign. To have a sound police department guarding the observance of rational laws, and by their very presence, quelling criminal action. It is not their position to dispense justice; it is only theirs to stop the use of force. Not to relieve their anxiety, but to use the minimum force necessary to restore the civil flow of society.

For one, what a relief it was to the country to see the 55 mph speed limit abolished. People could move again. High speed limits keep cities small. They allow civilization to spread out by bringing greater distances so much closer, which relieves congestion and improves business everywhere. Limits, if any, are to be determined in the road design by its ultimate sensible gauge: at what speed the populace chooses to travel it, so our officers can stop interrupting the flow and get back to real police work. It is our right and obligation to ensure that laws governing the roads are rational. To limit one's mobility is to limit one's effectiveness at self-sustenance, which only breeds dependency.

These are my rules for driving: 1) Don't get killed. Know your machine in adverse conditions and situations of aggressive recovery. 2) Be predictable. No swapping around mindlessly. Those who do so are typically in a hurry to get nowhere. 3) No contact, no foul. Hey, driving can be hell. No laws can harness the public to insure safety to the most lethargic. From the highest Self-made to the lowest Spirit Murderer, everyone is out there. Nothing is so socially competitive as traffic. Quick adjustments, smooth efficiency, honor, swift logical calm, furtive moral failure, hedonism, senseless aggression, you see it all. Traffic is a deliberate reflection of subconscious morality—people drive like they live.

Traffic and local ordinances aren't the only set of laws to be reexamined. Every regulation requires money subtracted from our pockets for its enforcement, so we should be as frugal as rationality permits. The concept of *fairness* recognizes and respects the choices and the results of those choices for every individual. Justice is done by maintaining proper credit or blame to those responsible for specific improvements or losses and holding harmless those not, in any realm. There are no victimless crimes that we should be wasting our time trying to collect fines against. For instance, the law needs to stay out of bedrooms and outside of any such *consensual* exchange between adults, homo or heterosexual, right or wrong. Legislators cannot peak in to inspect for moral consonance. Trying to legislate in areas that would require a KGB presence on every block and in every home just clogs up the works. We have to trust the citizens until given a specific reason not to, and invest our attention and public money elsewhere.

Sound Foreign Policy

America should treat nations like we treat friends, neighbors, or bullies, in response to how they act. The lending ratios used in an individual life are the same for a country. We shouldn't lend what we can't afford to lend, and what they can't afford to pay back. We must guarantee our own health if ever we need to step outside our boundaries to help those in need or to counter an irrational force. Nothing we do for another country should ever be bad for ours. We should lend to friends and never to enemies. We should not *create* enemies by drawing nations into financial servitude. We should help others, but never when we don't trust the motives or policies of those in power. In that case, we should invest our aid in a different way; by charging high tariffs to deal with us, and if necessary, by toppling their regime and installing a civil republic.

When we see an unusual number of immigrants or defectors from a particular country, we know the people are not being treated fairly. We shouldn't burden our people with an ongoing cost of feeding, housing, and providing medical care for them. We should instead weigh the military investment to free their country, so they can enjoy prosperity and freedom without leaving their homes. We should impose trade tariffs on police states—*NOT* enter free trade agreements—with the express intention of taxing the corruptors. We can call their loans, deny them war materials, gas, and oil, and weaken their grasp on the noose they have around the necks of the people. Then, coordinated with those who wish to see their leadership made a moral, sound administration, we go in. Using *our* Bill of Rights (not the U.N.'s) as the template, we set up a new government and show the people what is now possible to them. Our investment will come back many-fold as we say goodbye to a liability and welcome a new productive nation into the realm of those free.

Third-party verification is invaluable to assure that all international relations are fair, and if not, that conduct in response is justified. The value of calming world tensions before assumptions are made and reactions get out of control should be obvious (see the start of World War 1).

But the U.N. is proper only as a forum to vent and expose international concerns. It of itself *has* no country and should have no army, *no currency,* and no authority over us. Its power should be limited to a combination of countries participating in any particular event which affects them. America should make free trade agreements *only* with nations who match our productive capacity by morally sound means. We should no longer be tolerant of countries whose premises promise to—but never lead to—life. We have to impose constant pressure to assure a canopy of peaceful, disciplined sanity for all to live under. America's proudest reputation has been that of safe harbor for all the people who seek it. Life and Earth are for those who *want* to live, and who practice living premises. Those who don't, we can make arrangements for...but it must be done above board.

Free Trade Agreements

Free-trade can mean *"unregulated commerce"* or it can mean *"take what you want without paying for it."* Those attempting deceit use one meaning for political cover, while they accomplish the other. Its result is that our markets are unprotected, allowing slave nations to trade without penalties for their human rights violations.

Free trade *does not* mean there are no tariffs between nations. Such coalitions as NAFTA and the World Trade Organization intentionally suppress that the point of free trade is first and foremost to see *the people* free.

To give a looter's government the right to trade with America on equal terms translates into windfall profits for any nation employing slaves. If immoral men in American corporations set up shop there, it's easy money; it is the perfect slave/master relationship. The slave nation's army keeps the prisoners in line and their government gets a cut, producing goods sold abroad—far away from the murders, the cries, and the filth. That translates into healthy profits on the glossy pages of quarterly reports for international companies and a supposedly better standard of living for Americans as it masks our true inflationary environment. This makes it impossible for honest corporations at home to compete and permits coercive American monopolies to exist in the slave nations—*outside* the range of our laws, while reinforcing the slave nation's uncivil regimes. This is the Spirit Murderer's idea of social progress.

Free trade was not meant to be a megalomaniac's benefit, but a *citizen's* benefit. Until and unless these agreements accomplish what the civilized world expects of them, and unless they are crafted openly and subject to public scrutiny, they should be abolished.

Immoral Foreign Policy

Iran, Iraq, Pakistan, Austria, Egypt, Russia, Lebanon, the Palestinian Territories... We have to wonder why so many nations hate America. In many instances it is due to envy and corruption itself, but unfortunately, there have been many victims of our great strength as well. Since America's inception, attempts have been made to subvert her every facet of wealth. Our armies, economic strength, and international influence have all been bent to serve evil in very powerful ways, all carefully kept from the public eye.

There are many thieving rich in the country who have no intention of honoring the Republic. They don't care who the President is or what format the citizenship has voluntarily agreed to. They want whatever their interests lean towards and will commit any atrocity to influence those outcomes. Such men are consumed by the psychotic pursuit of dominance—the cognitive replacement for an esteem and stature their wealth has not given them—a vacuum filled by a vehement wrath towards all those who do not bend to their will.

War at its worst is letters to parents in one room, accounts receivable in the other. This is the Spirit Murderer's kind of artificial business—the *sure thing*, with devastation as gravy. But the covert side is much more sinister. We live the dream as Americans in this land of opportunity, and wonder how anyone rational could hate such a place. The media fuels this obvious lapse of reason while the true controversy remains hidden. We would be shocked to find the conspiracies to be true: families being murdered; towns and villages ransacked with their land and resources being given, not just to oil companies, but to *individuals* in our own country. Such victims wouldn't experience America through our lifestyle. All they would know of it would be the helicopters overhead; the abductions, the Nazi-style purges, the drug wars, and the political assassinations. When the camps were opened at the close of WWII, the German people were stunned by the extent of Hitler's atrocities, and carried an immense guilt for what they unleashed upon the world. We have to ensure that Americans are never in for similar shocks. No, such things are not done in our spirit, but are they being done in our name? Is our foreign policy spreading conquest while *claiming* to spread freedom? By taking our eyes off our institutions, we are ominously vulnerable to earning the spite of many countries, and to atone, any chance of this happening must be constantly scrutinized, exposed, rectified, and the perpetrators dealt with harshly.

American Armed Forces

The purpose of an army is to protect its borders in order to safeguard its countrymen. The military's function is to protect its country from all domestic, foreign, and natural opposition such as civil outbreaks, invasions, storms, or epidemics by whatever means is appropriate in order to return a secure, peaceful state of existence for its citizens. We as civilians delegate our use of physical force to the armed services to represent us in foreign and domestic issues. The question to ask is who decides when the use of force is proper?

The military is going to want to do what they were trained for, but they must submit to the coolest heads who steer the nation politically. Military men will have their own political ideas—everyone believes they can do the job better than those elected—but the tail cannot wag the dog. A body lives by the direction instructed by its head; not from an arm or a leg. Our political leadership is just as essential as our armies. Armies are the body, policy is the brain. In leaving office, President Eisenhower said, *"We must never let the military-industrial complex endanger our liberties or democratic processes."* He said it for a good reason, as it killed his successor. Unfortunately, history has shown how evil those in power can be, but it isn't always so. Rationality can return, as morality is what drives policy. Despite occasional abuses, we have by far the most moral internal and external civilian and military force on the planet, and they deserve our support. How many other countries use tear gas and rubber bullets when possible?

Still, as military personnel, always side with the people. If you see the citizens running for their lives, *from you,* you are no longer their protector. You are on the wrong side and it is your leaders who must go. Think of the long-term good for America—peace and freedom for all, oppression by none—and use your weapons wisely.

Voluntary Service

There is a difference in public reaction to a civilian death versus a military death. We emotionally factor in that possibility for military personnel, given the risk involved in their occupation versus what one would expect to encounter in private life. Military personnel and police officers should be well compensated for that potential—materially and spiritually. First and foremost, they should always have a choice of whether or not to serve in such a manner, including for whom and for how long. Volunteer armies are always the strongest, and there are just as many responsibilities to be addressed at home if some choose not to fight. If the man next to me is not committed, I don't want my life in his hands. If he can't handle it, he shouldn't be here (and probably won't be for long). Let him support the war effort as a citizen, being useful in his own way; there is no shame in that. Let him object until he understands the issue at stake. No man should die for a principle he has not acquired. No man has the right to push another out onto a battlefield; it is a direct Constitutional violation of our right to life.

Sacrifice is leaned on mostly in troubled times, but it can become an abusive political instrument. No one wants to sacrifice—ever; and they are right not to want to. Great care must be exercised before political leaders decide to risk one single human life. If we were threatened with invasion, I would fight without question, even knowing my chances of survival were not good. Resistance to aggression parallels the resistance to death that nature requires of us every day; such a tribute to life is not a sacrifice. But to be forced to go and die for some dubious cause is a national disgrace, and suspicious intentions always surround those who advocate a draft.

War is a minus-sum game to the mass citizenry—a pure expense in money and blood. Every building built, every creation brought into existence adds to our wealth, as does the steady economic state necessary to maintain it. War just destroys it all, generating nothing but cost. No one benefits from war. No one wants to spend more than necessary, unless some intend to profit by it. "Military businessmen" need a steady state of war; a direct contradiction to the steady state of peace needed by the citizenry. Throughout history, this fatal pursuit of profitability through violence has spread imperialism across the globe by one superpower after another. A company's military divisions should be a self-sustaining industrial obligation, *not* a key profit center. Our proper foreign efforts are to assure protection and justice to our citizenry abroad, never to assist them in gaining property for themselves by military means. We must protect only what has been acquired by voluntary trade.

The leaders who stem conflict at the cost of the fewest human lives are the greatest of heroes. The best solve issues on moral grounds without ever firing a shot. As we must defend ourselves, this is not always possible, so we do counter aggression vigorously. The greatest men in government gear foreign policy to ensure a safe world for all of us to venture into, and they work to spread the *basic means* of that freedom to all governments, who should want the same for their people. Not that their citizens must abandon their cultures or a modest life to pursue the American way of toasters and cars and homes, but simply that they are protected from coercion by their government and fellow citizens; not subjected to it. When their government could care less about their people, we make them pay to trade with us, or refuse them altogether. *That* is the moral reason for tariffs—to deny slave labor any advantage over our ethically run enterprises. There was a time when these tariffs paid for the entire cost of our government. We should seek this budget solution again.

Look at any totalitarian or socialist government and you will see few loyal soldiers, but many eventual defectors. Until the second Bush administration, no one defected from America. In our culture, every man's life is valuable. Every man has the right to live without subordinating his desires to anyone, and that is a land worth protecting—worth fighting for—worth dying for if necessary. If it came down to it, most Americans are willing to die for what America *is*—not for what it promises to be. The men of communist countries are considered expendable and are always left to die for *"the noble ideal,"* ideals which their fundamental premises make impossible. Americans don't have to create illusions about their country's potential greatness to be proud of; our culture makes it great. It is the nearest to Atlantis the world has ever been.

Chapter Seven

Aligning Our Strengths

History has shown the sides that follow to be antagonists, but in actuality, they are *perspectives*. America offered its citizens a greater promise: to rise above the chains, cultures and customs of the past and create a new world. This new world was based on *ideals;* not on present circumstances, but on how things could be and *ought* to be. It was an opportunity to reevaluate the tools we had, design a new destiny and build our way to the stars. Some forged ahead, jumping into the melting pot to achieve the success their courage deserved. Let's join them. It is *never* too late for the rest of us to take this leap.

The Sexes

Women needn't feel inadequate relative to men. A lesser physical power is *not* a sign of lower worth, but the simple mechanics of calculating the forces present. If you encountered a stampeding elephant or a speeding car, do you try to reason with it, or get out of the way? The essential difference between men and women is physical, but their cognitive power is *identical,* and cognitive power encompasses the majority of an individual's worth. Still, when push comes to shove, men *are* designed to be stronger.

By emulating male traits, feminists arrive at a miserable pseudo-equality that is of no greater value to anyone. Women's Libbers carry the sin of cognitive collusion—that *others* define them, that others must deal with them in a tailored way or their glass world is in jeopardy. They claim productive women should be a part of their cause, but what they sell them is an inferiority complex—believing they must convince every contrasting opinion and fight every transgression. Not to dodge every obstacle, but to be tripped up by every one of them. Why live in tension against unchangeable facts instead of expanding the range of what one *does* have and *can* build on?

The gender roles of protector and procreator will always exist; they are mankind's very moral-biological foundation. The value both genders bring to the table should not be spoken of as being of greater or lesser importance; both are *essential,* and women typically have the longer-range perspective. This depth is critical for us all to understand the greater impact our actions have on the world.

In the working world, integration is the answer, where everyone gets to witness the fact of our like cognitive power for itself. Equal pay for equal work is of course deserved, but should be *quit* over, not sued for. Our incapacity to judge our chances, a bad joke, or a crass comment does not justify a transfer of our assets to you. Be a man! Just deal with it.

The Social Classes

There are four financial classes of society: 1) the productive rich, 2) the productive middle, 3) the thieving rich and 4) the loafing poor (outside of political oppression, productive people do not stay poor). Every rational man agrees that no one should be paid for doing nothing, and yet the two latter classes have legal sanction to get away with it. These two are of the exact same rat mindset, and once moral men are out of the way, they are free to split powers, profits, and privileges between themselves and leave the populace to starve.

While struggling to make ends meet, the American middle class has always been considered the richest vat to prey upon by corrupt men. Every day, new laws are passed to place a larger burden on our shoulders while they placate us with budget controls. Spirit Murderers often disguise themselves as vanguards, preaching anti-life or dependency premises, which only necessitate the parasitism and destruction of other men. They have no tolerance to think, to judge or to weigh rational principles, wishing instead to point, shoot, and seize. Fear-driven organizations are designed around the centralization of confiscated energy's dispersal—a *mix* of cognition and interaction—to complete the *individual* living structure. They portray the masses as feeble and helpless and use our compassion to seek control over everyone. They preach that no man can survive alone, and prove it by destroying all those who try. Their laws are designed to penalize independent traits to the extent that we exemplify them. While they withhold acknowledgement of our moral value in order to harness us, they have been busy setting up channels for our prosperity.

This pattern quickly assumes the shape of Socialism, and the classes eliminated are the productive rich and the productive middle. The thieving rich reign and everyone else is condemned to poverty and squalor. At a time when our economy is falling apart, CEO's are still taking incomes 262 times higher than their average employee, yet the enterprise—which is their duty to secure—is left financially unsound. They attempt to justify such outrageous compensation as necessary to tempt beings of practically "sainted" abilities, but this is folly; it is clear that pirates are in control again and must be removed.

Only once in history were there men at the top who set up a system that did not provide them with a cut of our lives in return, but served the longer range profit of a free, stable, productive industrial society. The birth of America marked the birth of two new social classes of honor, and they must be preserved. This *is* the class war between the Self-made and the Fear-driven in economic terms. With a new moral philosophy to guide us, perhaps this time the thieving rich and the loafing poor can join the endangered species list, as they deserve.

Self-Defense and Gun Control

Though the media does all it can to rile the public into thinking America is going to hell in a hand basket—that crime is rampant and getting worse—the reality is far different. Their motto is *"If it bleeds, it leads"*, so the first thing we hear about is murders and violent crimes (my rule for the news: upon the report of a third crime, I turn it off). Statistics show that over the last 20 years in America, property crimes are down over 20%, homicides are down over 30%, and car thefts are down over 40%. Perhaps news producers are so unimaginative they simply cling to this concept to hold the audience, and as a result, totally misrepresent the moral condition and progress of our country. Or perhaps there is a more sinister force at work.

Instead of offering such reassuring stats, what do we hear? High profile crimes with large body counts—real or staged—coupled with immediate attacks on our right of self-defense (the Second Amendment). The media generates such an aura of crisis that the citizens feel, *"Oh my god, children are being killed every day! We have to do something!"* And what they do is get stampeded into disarming themselves to show their devotion to peace—forgetting to weigh the motives behind the defensive versus offensive use of *any* weapon—surrendering the country to potential mass murder to follow.

"...with devotion's visage and pious action we do sugar on the Devil himself." -William Shakespeare

So if the disintegration of civility in America isn't real, what is the purpose and urgency of disarming us?

Regarding the grim prospect of invading the United States in WW2, Japanese Admiral, Isoroku Yamamoto, is claimed to have said, *"There would be a rifle behind every blade of grass."* True, there are over 300 million privately owned firearms in the U.S. It isn't invading forces we need fear, it is our own internal enemies: the Spirit Murderers responsible for our degrading health and economic collapse. Our Oath of Allegiance warns us: we must defend the Constitution *"against all enemies, foreign and domestic."* It should say "the Constitution *and* the people."

Criminals know to stay away from armed people and communities, preferring to prey on those more vulnerable. Sharks attack sick and struggling fish that can't fight back, minimizing the risk of injury to themselves. Their senses are designed to detect weakness—it *lures* them—the scenario is innate in nature, and this is true for fear-driven politicians and empty plutocrats as well. This is a constant throughout the animal kingdom: the young, the old, the weak, the sick, they are all targets for predation. Weapons and armor improve their chances of survival. Giving up our guns *reduces* our chances for survival, and against an organized enemy, eliminates it.

Self-government and self-defense go hand in hand. No regime can provide 24/7 protection. With an average of 17 police officers for every 10,000 American citizens, the citizens must maintain the capacity to police themselves. Take away this right and the productive are sitting ducks for the destructive. Politicians may say, *"To secure law and order, we will confiscate all guns"*, but this will not secure law and order; it never has and it never will. It only assures guns will not be aimed at them. Life or death for citizens can then be chosen with little risk to the power structure, and their choice is always death. Granted such a victory, they quickly drop the illusion that they are working for the people and reveal the truth: that the people are at their mercy, to be disposed of at their whim. Why? Because, left with sticks and stones, the people are no longer a threat. They surrendered any comparable means to defend themselves and can now be pushed around, put to work, or punished inhumanly, and will have to endure it or face their master's ultimate argument.

"To disarm the people is the best and most effectual way to enslave them."
-George Mason, father of the American Bill of Rights

In his web article "Gun Control Dictator Style - Tyrants Who Banned Firearms Before Slaughtering The People", Bradlee Dean commented, *"How ironic that those who are calling for gun control are those who want the guns so they can have the control."* Dean then documented the statements and actions of the world's most devastating butchers, and those they considered a threat.

"All political power comes from the barrel of a gun. The communist party must command all the guns, that way, no guns can ever be used to command the party." —Mao Tze Tung

As a result of establishing gun control in China, Mao's forces were able to round up 20 million political dissidents *without a fight* and exterminate them.

"To conquer a nation, first disarm its citizens." -Adolph Hitler

As a result of establishing gun control in Germany, Hitler's forces were able to round up 13 million Jews and political dissidents *without a fight* and exterminate them.

"Death solves all problems–no man, no problem."
-Joseph Stalin

As a result of establishing gun control in the Soviet Union, Stalin's forces were able to round up 20 million dissidents *without a fight* and exterminate them.

"To keep you is no benefit. To destroy you is no loss." -Pol Pot

Pol Pot killed over one million citizens of Cambodia; civil, educated, disarmed people who were killed just for being intelligent, or if you can believe it, simply *looking* intelligent. No one so callous to the value of human life should be in power longer than it takes to discover it.

Why would we trust the representatives of a government with immense military power who do not wish to permit its citizens the same self-protection? Law-abiding citizens properly supplement the police and military. The only reason to disarm them is to extend control over and ultimately dispose of them. The cost of military intervention into public matters is so high, by far the easiest solution is to arm the citizens directly and have them handle civil defense. Many countries require military training. According to federal statute, most of us are in fact considered members of the reserve militia of the United States, and in towns such as Kennesaw and Nelson, Georgia, citizens are *required* to own guns. Have crimes skyrocketed in such places? No, it has plummeted. The vast majority of American citizens who own guns do so for protection and recreation; they do not *live* by the gun. They live productive lives and can be trusted to defend not only themselves, but infused with a fierce sense of justice, will often risk themselves to save those in harm's way. In the worst scenario, an armed populace serves as a check to illegitimate power if ever an attempt is made to use the military, or a private mercenary force, against the people.

The US military had a hard time dealing with a guerrilla war in Iraq with 30 million inhabitants. A guerrilla war against 300 million inhabitants is unwinnable. Most of our military personnel would join the citizens anyway, once they realized their corrupt leaders expected them to kill American families like their own.

Why would they take such a step? Desperation. Human health has proven too resilient. It's just that, once you have killed all the bees and that didn't work, stopped the North Atlantic current and that didn't work, dumped toxic heavy metals on people and that didn't work, foisted man-made diseases, banned cures, poisoned citizens through their food supply and personal products and that didn't work, at some point the corrupt rich will resort to bullets to pare the population down to their magic number.

With guns, we are citizens. Without them, we are subjects, which is a nice way to say slaves. Do not let them take our guns in the midst of a voluntary, civil exchange, because after that, they risk nothing if they choose to be uncivil, which is what history has proven fear-driven governments do, time and time again. If they come for your guns and ammunition, make sure they get the bullets first.

"The end of democracy and the defeat of the American Revolution will occur when government falls into the hands of lending institutions and moneyed incorporations."
-Thomas Jefferson, 1816

In 2010, Jesse Ventura filmed hundreds of thousands of plastic coffins accumulating near the CDC in Atlanta. Who do you think those coffins are for? The old money men behind our government are immensely dangerous to the future of mankind. The useless descendants of industrialists and barons, they have degenerated so badly that they see no way forward unless everyone else dies.

Their Georgia Guidestones state this clearly: a world population goal of 500 million maximum. Given any social problem, murder is always their answer. They are NOT their great grandparents: *no greatness remains*, and their money has become a cancer, metastasizing through channels of the like-minded. We have to protect ourselves against them, assert our right to exist on this planet, and contain or eliminate their influence, just as they would choose to eliminate us. These sick, demented, atrociously wealthy individuals have no greater right to this planet than we do. Any concentrations of capital attempting social or political control should be policed carefully and in most cases barred or seized. Anyone linked to America's genocidal puzzle should be prosecuted, jailed for life, or executed.

American Megalomania Exposed: Mass Coffins in Atlanta

A group of people with weapons is a potential army to be reckoned with. A group of people with no weapons is a malleable workforce to be exploited, thinned, or eliminated. Don't be the person held by your hair, pushed down to your knees and shot to death while some nonviolent (as of yet) morally uncertain young subject records it with their iPhone. Don't be the person, in your last moments, stunned and regretful that you gave up your guns, and that this—what you never thought the government you trusted would do to you—disbelieving right up to the bang, that this is your fate. The irony is, it may be your gun! You, who would never fire your weapons unless you or your family was in danger, are being delivered to your death by a regime that does not honor the same values—only using them as a mask. Worse yet, your family may be on their knees beside you. Together, we can change this fate for our people. Faith in a false peace is faith in fantasy. It is an illusion that destroys all values eventually, and there are no do-overs once you wake up. Wake up now. Better men wanted to assure that you were not subject to such tyrannical motivations. Honor them by fighting for your rights, in mind, body, and spirit.

"A free people ought not only be armed and disciplined, but they should have sufficient arms and ammunition to maintain a status of independence from any who might attempt to abuse them, which would include their own government."

–George Washington

So is it time to fight back?

Unsafe vaccines … Suppressed cures … Murdered doctors … 80,000 untested chemicals in our food, health, and beauty products … Food supply monopolies and gestapo tactics … Media monopolies … Money supply monopolies and national bankruptcy … Financing our enemies while our own soldiers die … Energy monopolies … CDC pathogen satellites and concentration camps nationwide … Toxic nano-metals raining down from the sky…

It has been time to fight back since objective evidence in any important regard was not acted on. Since profit was chosen as a priority over health. Since quarterly reports were given preference to the safety of children. Since frightening preparations were initiated. Self-made Americans need to recognize that we are in a constant state of war against such influences, and these people must be dealt with harshly. Stand tall and deliver ultimatums, or you are just a beggar. In seeking reforms, offer not only objective evidence and a proper course of action expected, but clear and decisive threats of civil disobedience and *immediate* follow-through: the corrupt are motivated by nothing less. Boycott specific businesses, one at a time, issue by issue. Boycott industries. Don't take *"NO"* for an answer. *The People's* posture needs to be "Do the right thing *or else*". *Force change* or be laughed at behind closed doors.

Should civil war come once more in America, it will likely be a result of defaulting on our national debt. Once money dries up for public assistance—sustenance for those who make excuses rather than working for a living—they will begin to openly prey on the honorable working class. Nothing you have will be safe. Crime will skyrocket as they starve. Alternatively, so great a burden will be placed on the middle class that working itself will no longer be a road to prosperity; incentives for a moral life will be extinguished and a new Dark Age will ensue. What can we expect when a great mass is permitted to exist without educations, dimmed and inept to the most basic elements of self-sufficiency? Why should we carry those who are of no use—not to us or themselves—and never intend to be?

If it comes down to a fight, the corrupt rich and the thieving poor *have to lose.* America is ours. Its laws, its ideals, its Forefathers; all reflect our deepest values—values that run contrary to all the monopolists and do-nothings stand for. Do not go silently into that good night. Do not give up the rich culture we have created and the bright future we deserve.

Fostering Ethnic Accord

There is perhaps no greater spiritual war or a more false endeavor than the pursuit of racial superiority. Those *for* racial solidarity lose their best to the torrent of capitalist freedom, were anyone can be anything they are willing to work towards, breaking ethnic borders as a side effect. The most dynamic sweep aside such inessentials in their upward surge to fulfillment. For that, we must leave the nest and its cohesive safety and focus purely on human essentials—those of all humans, not just our own race or culture—and market our wares to the world. The backward people cannot dismiss their culture; they hang onto it like Linus hangs onto his blanket. Producing no unique identity of their own, they cling to it for identity. Supposedly a symbol of pride, it is actually quite the opposite. Instead of engaging in personal growth, they try to reverse the process, looking into their background for attributes to bring forward and accentuate. Fear to venture out becomes identity crisis, which becomes false pride and a border *not* to be crossed. While many minorities fail to dissolve inessential differences in the melting pot of integration, America's key race issue has always been between white and black.

Most people imagine African life as television has portrayed it—as a primitive people with no technology, practicing religious rituals even more senseless and irresponsible than ours. They believe blacks were simply taken from places where they ran mindlessly through the jungle, but the truth is their homes were settlements not much different from the American colonies at the time. All civilizations have unique rituals, but most of their time was spent as ours is now: working for the common maintenance of life. Their villages were ransacked and their people were taken. Imagine that happening to us today by another nation, or to individuals who are abducted—their very lives stolen—a nightmare for anyone.

Slavery was brought to the New World in the 1600's, spreading from the Caribbean colonies of European States and South America, but it was a part of human history from the beginning. America *inherited* slavery—we didn't create it. From the start, slavery was acknowledged as a blatant violation of her true principles. The Founding Fathers had a choice: accepting slavery in the southern States and facing Britain together, or drop the ideal of a unified country. The South refused to ratify the Constitution otherwise. Our Founders did it right; they allowed America to develop its own sovereign inertia before abolishing key impurities with time and pressure. The honorable men of that time did the best they could.

Ultimately, the unsound economic policies of The South put the whole country in jeopardy, allowing European financial interests to prey on their foolishness, intending to split the nation and give the halves back to England and France, which spurred the American Civil War and an end to slavery. Since then, integration has been difficult. In Ancient Egypt, the slaves left. America chose the hardest way—learning to trust one another. It was the right thing to do. Now look how far we have come; America's first black president *elected by a landslide*, chosen simply because he was the best man for the job. And with him, new hope: for peace; for the return of our freedoms; for the dawn of an enduring prosperity.

With this reawakening of the American spirit, we all have a new pinnacle to aspire to. But in defining ourselves, should we be limited by nation, race, or family? Our link to historical pride is in the traits we honor and wish to practice. Who from the past (or present) reflects your views? *Spiritual* lineage is infinitely more significant than physical; we can all project ourselves alongside our heroes and strive to deserve their stature. We are most intimately, descendants of those we admire.

People can be divided any number of ways—nations, races, families, genders—but the division stops at individuals. The cognitive process of men and women of all races is identical, and its disciplined adherence is the moral measure of all. Race is just one element of who we are. True identity—our soul and fullest moral potential—is defined by our deepest parallel: our like cognitive power, and our willingness to use it. It's your life. What are *you* doing to make it better?

Fostering Religious Accord

Most people are far too decent for the morality they have been subjected to. When we contemplate how we live and how we affect others in the process, we want to be viewed positively. This is why many cling to the cultural standard, even if they see it being misused.

Have you ever explored a topic and though having many elements defined, still could not put a finger on a thing's essence? You make an assumption upon which all of your calculations are based, but something's off. Eventually you identify the source of your inquest, and calculating from there, everything works out. It is the same with moral judgment. When you replace the many claimed sources with the nature of existence, everything falls into place.

As a people, we suffer the bipartisan animosity reared by this moral confusion: the unthinking side rigidly following popular morality in haughty righteousness, while independent people dismiss its many ludicrous hassles, and with good reason. What rationality prevents, religion permits. Religion has shown what a free reign of its supremacy would mean in the medieval savagery of the Dark Ages, and the paranoid horror of the Salem witch trials. No one wants to get bogged down in another period of mystic ooze. Without an alternative path leading to moral stability, we have stayed in low gear, spiritually. What has been missing is context, and what makes the riddle of morality clear is the earned versus the unearned; the deserved versus the confiscated; the life-furthering versus the life-destroying.

Heaven and Earth

In childhood, I was told that heaven was whatever I wanted it to be. But I wanted to *deserve* the world around me. *Ownership* through *earnership.* Why did they think I wanted it for free?

The immoral image of heaven or any utopia, is getting everything for nothing; never having to lift a finger. We see the practical result of that in slums, welfare offices, and in those who *do* pursue it, by pulling insurance jobs, staging accidents, and filing nuisance suits. We see it in Islamic Fundamentalism and Third-world slave states, yet an effortless existence is consistently glorified by religion—something no truly moral man would ever want. Pursuing their land flowing with milk and honey, as these are products of human effort, all they bring about is a land flowing with blood. Such people spend their lives chasing illusions, fatally loyal in treason to Earth and all those they encounter. This is not Divine Circumstance, but simple neurosis.

We hear, *"If this footstool is your heaven, you are not aiming very high."* They put down their flesh, their wants, their work, their relationships, and their lives. But in life they are a mind looping in panic. They consider reality to be beside the point, and the point is, *their wish.* They declare life to be senseless, and given the way they live, they are right. If life here doesn't matter, then why bother opposing those who live here and love it?

Hell

It has always been implied that we risk losing our souls if we question Fear-driven clergy, claiming that to defy *them* is to defy God. Often, such intimidating leaders can't convey anything without deserving to get maced. We are condemned for our daily greed in that hour-long commute, eight hours of disciplined focus, and that second hour-long commute. They leave us no chance, making us evil by birth (Original Sin). Look at a newborn; isn't it evil? It is Man: notice its fangs, its claws, and its violent intentions. Notice its black heart (sarcasm intended). Imagine the parents of a newborn froggy bearing down on him to say *"See those legs? If you were a decent frog, you wouldn't have to hop."* Or plant parents saying "If you were a decent plant, you wouldn't have to strive for water, light, and air. You wouldn't stretch out to greet its warmth, but be *humbled* under the sun." Pointing to an uprooted, dried and shriveled weed, they'd say "*That* is virtue before the Lord." Ridiculous and unnatural for other species, that is exactly what the Spirit Murderers have done to Man. The only black hearts are to be found in those who perpetrate such nonsense, grown men whom out of moral carelessness, tell children they are evil. We listen to their chaste of sacrifice, self-denial, humbleness, and repression, then get up the next morning and proceed to make all the right moves with no moral credit.

Independent judgment is held as spiritual treason, to be countered with the most horrific retributions in their afterlife. We are taught to trust in their guidance alone: the cornerstone of abject dependence and politically, of dictatorship.

There is no punishing a trait of all men and there is no preexisting human evil. Such an idea violates the very definition of morality—the *choice* to do good or evil, which also *requires* the freedom to choose. There should be no questioning of human capacities—only using them. Guilt should be attached to its proper cause: the unwillingness to carry our own burdens in life. Those who have interpreted Man as evil have given us their own *self*-estimate. There *is* no Hell, beyond what the Spirit Murderers make of life.

Warrior Note: *A guilt accused of all men leaves no benefactor to atone to.*

The Nature of Moral Leadership

Higher concepts in reason are a derivation of walking the chain of knowledge, but ill religious concepts lead from nowhere to universal harmony, without stopping to ask how. Their altruist fog permits ideals that bear no adherence to the 1-4 cognitive process below. Their true fantasy is where anything is possible *morally*, an anti-concept used to justify the slaughter of men and the seizure of our assets throughout history.

Objectivity *cannot* be subverted; there is no becoming a victim of reason. Rational concepts are intuitive of life. Instead, *dictated action* removes moral choice, and thus the pride it could generate. *Unsound faith* removes moral responsibility. Either approach taken by religion or the State creates drones—blind, deaf, and dangerous.

"Faith in the supernatural, begins as faith in the superiority of others." —Atlas Shrugged

Faith is confidence in the continuation of a known pattern. When used improperly, faith is meant not to enhance reason, but to avoid it. Their "higher state of being" doesn't bring what you first expect: a clearer understanding. No, it is a state where cognitive effort for understanding and physical effort for reward is unnecessary. A "higher mode of consciousness," *must* result not in a negation of your senses, but in greater clarity, building on what you already know.

But instead of working to acquire their prophet's heroic *human* traits, die-hard illusionists mimic their impossible marvels, reflecting the superhero worship of children which they show such contempt for. They want to raise their hands and part the sea, but refuse to define constructive means to overcome their barriers. They want to magically raise the dead or heal the sick, but won't listen to evidence that stems sickness and the patterns that lead to it. They will call upon the heavens to guide their lives, but won't hold their emotions in check to think clearly. They are willing to snap their fingers and turn one free meal into ten, but shrug at the moral constancy necessary to earn them, or anything else. They have a ruthlessly disciplined imagination, a one-way valve that closes at the first touch of reality. At any time, two key destinies lie before every man: the result of effort and that of sloth. Look down and see whose feet are moving. If they are yours, then so is the decision of where to place them.

A *morality* is an endeavor of Man like any other (such as medicine and computer technology), always in some stage of development, subject to constant scrutiny and continually being advanced, seeking to enhance the living power of individuals in the most spiritually profitable way. *That* requires an active mind to practice and to pass down.

Epi-stems and the Origin of Existence

The proper moral code is the same every morning you wake up. It never changes. Axioms *are,* and that's it. Finding the origin of the universe or even proof of a god will not change our sleep cycles, the due dates on our Visa bills, or absolve us of responsibility for our day-to-day lives. This is our life's context, whose effort is never to be escaped, jilted, or transferred to others.

So, can we become Christians and automatically gain superiority over those who are not? Accepting Jesus (or Allah for that matter) doesn't give one the knowledge to practice anything. It is a *pledge* to be virtuous—nothing more. A *proper* moral pledge is to actively pursue the *knowledge* necessary to be virtuous—the commitment to fully adhere to the rational process of cognition. And your success in this endeavor is your *actual* adherence and its result; the civil preservation and furtherance of life. *This* is the bridge between us all.

Warrior Note: *As language is a means of comprehension, it precedes and therefore negates religion as a substitute for comprehension.*

I can't imagine surrendering my faculties for an unobservable alternate universe when this one is as complex as it is. Its scope and implications are difficult to grasp with every weapon you have set to stun! And attaining *rational* conviction is a road nature defined for us each to travel alone.

Looking forward, the lost will persist in unquestioning obedience to maintain an image of moral adherence, never questioning the standard to which they adhere. Yet here is the real world to feel and hear and see, which encompasses the whole of their lives, is the subject of their every conscious moment *and makes possible* their contemplation of the nonexistent. The *true* field of their awareness has a consistent, non-contradictory structure identified by Man and *demonstrable*, step-by-step. It purely respects their means of cognition and gauges their advance with a clear link to the steps that come before and those to follow. All they need is the courage to see.

Conversations are an example of walking the epistemological chain. That is why in trying to apply it to life, religious conversations often end in violence or silence, even between believers. This is due to delusional fantasies borne of differing cognitive breaks. What one wants to believe differs from what the other wants to believe, but neither is held to the rules of thought, so no middle ground is possible.

Interpretation and Hypocrisy

Religion has made hypocrites out of people with sincere motives—those who sought no contradictions—a tragic result for an honest effort. There are two ways to see everything, and the anti-organic, anti-rational, anti-human choice is the evil choice. There is less and less need for martyrdom as a society grows more civil. As martyrdom is their symbol, to keep religion alive, they have to make sure society *doesn't* grow more civil. As Jesus indicated, we can choose the nature of Biblical interpretation ourselves. Those who negate the path to life are the *true* hypocrites.

Between Spirit Murderer and Self-made man, both seek to claim virtue, but use religion in very different ways. The loafers quote scripture that justifies stagnation and damns their betters, such as *"The meek shall inherit the Earth"*, *"Pride for wealth is the ultimate evil,"* and, *"It is easier for a camel to pass through the eye of a needle than for a rich man to enter the kingdom of heaven."* In Biblical times, men got rich *only* by over-taxation and plunder, so pride for wealth would have been one step above pride for murder. But shame doesn't apply to wealth earned in a free country where exchange is voluntary—*pride* does. In response, the productive quote scripture that justifies their effort and absolves their guilt. For example: *"Lord, thou deliveredst to me two talents: behold, I have gained two other talents besides them. His lord said unto him, Well done, thou good and faithful servant; thou hast been faithful over a few things, I will make thee ruler over many things: enter thou into the joy of thy lord."* —Matthew 25:23. Another servant buried his. He is told to give his money to the industrious servant and is condemned, *"cast ye the unprofitable servant into outer darkness: there shall be weeping and gnashing of teeth."* —Matthew 25:30. The lethargic strike back with more scripture, *"...he that is the greatest among you shall be your servant. And whosoever shall exalt himself shall be abased; and he that shall humble himself shall be exalted."* —Matthew 23:12. Still, this could mean damnation of a Spirit Murderer's social facade and approval of Self-made man's non-esteem seeking, wholesome encounters with others. A sanction of rational self-interest and capitalist freedom can be found in *"Is it not lawful for me to do what I will with my own?"* —Matthew 20:15. Did Jesus tell us to violate our minds? *"Blessed are those who believe without seeing"* could be interpreted as blind faith, or as a sanction of abstraction. Moral *validation* of our senses can be found in *"...blessed are your eyes, for they see: and your ears, for they hear."* —Matthew 13:16. The talent story sanctions the proper value hierarchy of Man, as does the following: *"Let all things be done decently and in order."* —1st Corinthians 14:40.

There is a whole different way to interpret The Bible if you love being alive. Both sides seek moral cover that reflects their ends, but one needs cover and one doesn't. One is a fear-ridden, parasitical slacker whose guilt is valid, while the other's guilt is contrived. The full context of most Bible stories promotes mutual respect, civility, and hard work, dissolving the intention of a Spirit Murderer's malicious snippets. With the process of cognition known, it is clear what they are doing. Your own conscience must decide which pattern to follow.

Regardless of a person's argument, you can feel who intends to leave you with less. When interpretation must be pitted against objectivity, one side intends to preserve predatory slaughter as an alternative to civility. If any natural part of your body or mind is negated, *run*. It is all there for a reason, and that reason *exposes* their moral corruption. You can also feel who is interested in your well-being. He brings you new knowledge to contemplate; he doesn't try to commandeer your will or shut you down.

Self-made men don't teach *"Believe me or else,"* they teach *"See for yourself."* Philosophically, I can see the grid system of my work charted out into the future. I can see it superimposed over the past, and how and where the Bible lessons fit. There *is* a sanction of life and rationality to be found at different cognitive levels of its contexts. I can see its long-term intention to *integrate* moral knowledge, where most present interpretation lends itself to *disintegration.* Learn the grid and the narrow path is no longer so.

Jesus's True Contribution

Jesus was a man devoid of pretense. He had the mark of genius so rare in any time—someone who had reached full volitional consciousness—yet he had to depend on average minds to record and carry his message. Had he lived longer, I'm sure he would have taken his work to the next level. He would have resolved its existential contradictions, clarified the true essence of evil, and made what he preached more palatable for all. Instead, given the unexplained implications in his word, interpretation was left to those also lacking a proper standard of value from which to extract sound meaning. They relied on that period's cultural standard, with the Submission/Domination Axis as their only reference and key moral conflict. Their solution was to turn the tables and become the dominant, and sacrifice was therefore perpetuated.

Jesus was at odds with the law and at odds with the church. He didn't think the law was helping the people. He didn't think the church was guarding their faith. They were envious. They wanted the love of those he drew voluntarily, and they still want it. Like Judas attempting to exploit his following, they were eager to silence him in order to put words in his mouth. Diminishing the power of the church by fostering independent spirituality was a massive threat to them. The message in his death was "Don't give up your morality. Die for it if necessary, knowing it *is* a question of life or death." By standing mute and adding nothing of his own, he showed what the rulers were all about. Challenging the trust of one divine leader for interpretation versus God being in *every* man—*this* was Jesus' revelation, and one step closer to the truth of *moral* empowerment. For a power seeker, there is no greater threat. If morality was to be an attribute of the individual, next to follow would be self-government and they would be dethroned. They were.

The Medieval Truth

"My karma ran over your dogma." —bumper sticker

Religions have been used through time as a license to torture. There isn't a moral action they don't have a penalty for; there isn't a moral violation they are not guilty of. Whether purported now or 2000 years ago, a Spirit Murderer is behind every choice against the flow of natural life. Their job is to stop, condemn, sentence, and drag people to their deaths—their historic constant. Give them control even now, and their intentions would have the same medieval end.

I suffered their doctrines as a child, and the unbelievable violence. We had to memorize what we were expected to believe. Like learning to smoke, we had to ignore the convulsions and pretend we loved it. Only those who used lies to pursue plunder were good at it. To them, evasions came natural; from generation to generation it was the continual rebirth of the Socratic Method; of Apartheid; of the Spanish Inquisition. "*Kill your body to free your soul. Accept your own worthlessness. Obey us because only we are privileged to interpret the unknowable. Trust no outsider. Damn enjoyment, damn progress, damn ability. Our perfect world of peace is a cemetery. We will never run out of victims, because someone will always want to live.*"

I submit to you, that it was not a god who told you to violate your own nature—who said you can't think, that you can't protect yourself, that you must allow your life and happiness to be sacrificed and that you are guilty when you have done nothing wrong. It was not a god that told you to spit in your own face, but fear-based men.

Warrior Note: *The good determined by any standard other than life will achieve its opposite.*

The infamy is that if your guardians could start a new world from scratch, *this* is what they would teach that world with the cross as their symbol; as if to say, "*Blood sacrifice: that is all you need to know."* Trust no dogma whose symbol is death! Only when their actions reflect their savior, *not* his killers, can we take them seriously. It is not so important how Jesus died. What is important is how he lived. When they return such a great man to the proper setting of life and worship *that,* we will know they are on the right path.

At this point in our history, I can't help but feel that the morally-devoted of all faiths *are* starting down the path to life and freedom for all. I sense this is the result of good people pursuing healthy guidance, who have approached the building of their highest self with the most innocent of motives, yet have been betrayed by immense and all-pervading financial and political corruption worldwide. They know something has to change. They are learning that the faith they grant to their god cannot be transposed to our leaders, whose actions must pass the deepest and clearest scrutiny. Paraphrasing Bram Stoker, "We must not let our eyes see nor our ears hear, that which we cannot account for."

Man's Savior

Imagine going to confession and knowing you have no sins to confess. That state of guiltless purity is quite a sensation and quite a worthy goal, but the price is full volitional awareness—the lifelong commitment to stand naked before the truth of cognitive evidence. I won't tell you that you can practice the opposite just by claiming it is right for you, and prosper with an approach that is contrary to life. Follow the rational process of cognition and you will not be confused. You will not be taken advantage of, and you will not be immoral. Instead, you will generate the most profound and lasting pride, never to be surrendered again. Face the world alone. Look to *existence* for the answers you seek, and as He said, "*Turn over a stone, and you will find me.*"

The Transformation of Christianity

Most Americans consider themselves Christians, but they do many things Christ would not have done. He wasn't excluding people right and left or shunning his enemies; he was drawing people together. But there are 34,000 different Christian sects, all based on disagreements: 34,000 groups thinking what they want to think and shutting themselves off from everyone else. If you are a Christian, you shouldn't see yourself as a group opposed to other groups. You should try to be more like *Jesus was!* He was peaceful, independent, and confident enough to be open. But in reaching out to the Church, wishing to share these cognitive structures and the moral certainty they offer, I have found it mostly to be a closed door. In less civil times, when Jesus began to speak, the townspeople tried to push him off a cliff. If we keep holding up these barriers, nothing will change.

The Christian audience is the most important audience on Earth, because the fate of the free world is in their hands. Christianity must lead the charge, and transform into a purely nature-respecting philosophy. Invite me in, and I will help you. America and all free nations *must* show a united front to the world, and I submit that the moral code we can all agree on can only come from nature itself.

This is not a radical expectation. Back in the thirteenth century, St. Thomas Aquinas discovered the works of Aristotle. Aquinas wrote extensively on the subject, and was so persuasive that the Catholic Church absorbed the full works of Aristotle into the Christian faith. The work of Aristotle lies at the base of ALL major religions, serving as the *rational, acceptable* part. His work can even be found in Muslim teachings since the seventh century. Only a morality's *practical* value can make it stick. Historically, the resounding undercurrent of truth upsets all contrary designs.

By describing the natural patterns we *all* practice, *Moral Armor* has advanced the work of Aristotle, drawing a deeper moral parallel between men than has ever existed. St. Thomas Aquinas would be first to champion the seamless integration of nature and moral devotion. So you see, it has happened once already. It is time for Christianity to show its leadership and take another brave step.

Now, understand that no one has to give up their religion. There are no demands made here; *Moral Armor* is just an acute observation of natural law, and its simple yet profound moral structure. The beauty is, we live by this philosophy already, and it is critical to be able to confirm true moral premises through nature. *Knowing* is much more powerful than leaving things to faith. On the world stage, you have to stick to what you can prove. Allegiance to life must come before religious or political ideas. If your ideas do not honor the peaceful, biological furtherance of an individual, if they disrupt or deny life to mankind, then *they are wrong.*

If you are truly interested in being the best person you can be, you should constantly be learning from *every* available source. With the structures I have outlined, you will end up with a practically clairvoyant understanding of your own religion, and that goes for *any* religion or philosophy in history. You can lay the grid over it and see precisely where they are right or wrong and where their lessons fit.

Most of us, Christian and otherwise, are *already* practicing nature's morality—it is the silent undercurrent in life that binds us all—we just need explicit awareness of it. Once you are *openly* aware and your motives are all flowing in one common, life-furthering direction, you will gain an overwhelming confidence and a spiritual fulfillment beyond anything you could imagine. People will notice life blooming around you, and it will spread by example alone. Your kids will be on track to living confident, productive, happy lives and most of your worries will be gone. So take a deep breath and be brave. Give nature's morality a chance because we can't win without you. If your religious premises are sound, then they will flow *with* life, and never against it. By honoring our common ground, free civilizations will be unbeatable. By morally empowering every individual, we will achieve what Jesus intended anyway, and then *world* peace is just a matter of time.

Chapter Eight

American Challenges

Of course, not everything is perfect in America. Here at the beginning of the 21st century, our republic is threatened on many fronts. While some issues are the responsibility of corrupt men in the echelons of power, others are under our control. Ultimately, *all* are ours to fight if we want our country back. Here is what I consider our most dangerous vulnerabilities:

Single Mothers and Fatherless Children

When children are not planned by two dedicated people in love, they become an ominous cloud over America's future. Three instances come to mind, which threaten our integrity and freedom more effectively than most any other issue. Let's start with welfare.

A conspiring couple may say "The government will give us $X for the production of each baby. The government wants babies! If we control costs and push the remaining burden onto the shoulders of others, we won't have to work!" Obviously the thought-process of the lowest substratum, do we really want to expand it? Of course it is folly to imagine this couple would stay together for the children. Such people live without deep values. Love and commitment are fleeting, so they quickly separate. Welfare pays for up to seven children; does anyone see a trend in that most welfare moms have seven kids before showing any self-discipline regarding their pregnancies? With responsible, self-supporting couples producing two children on average every 20-30 years, the lethargic, careless, and uneducated are outpacing us by more than 3 to 1, and with the geometric progression of their fifteen-year generation cycle, it is *much worse* than that. Since welfare was instituted it has become a full-blown epidemic. In 1960, only five percent of births were out of wedlock. Today, *thirty-five percent* of all births in America are illegitimate. The acceleration of the trend and its implications are so horrific, I can barely summon the courage to contemplate it.

What about accidental cases, such as when teens get pregnant? Both the boy and girl involved are just scared kids themselves. Most often, the boy panics and runs as he is *far* from prepared for children and family. If she chooses to keep the child, she has committed herself to care for another for longer than she has even been alive. With no education and no means of livelihood, *seventy-seven percent* of teen mothers are on welfare within five years of the child's birth. Unfortunately she transfers this plight and her family enters the cycle of poverty, as children raised on welfare are seven times more likely to become dependent on welfare than are other children.

Last are women who intentionally trap men. We constantly hear of crackdowns on "dead-beat dads," but the topic of how they often originate remains hidden and deserves serious light: *Dead-beat Mothers.* Defaulting on life, her goal is to have her future assured—to force a man into a position where he no longer has a choice but to support her. Trapping a spouse is among the worst long-range acts of malice, as it permanently affects so many; the child most of all. It usually backfires anyway; over 80% of the time, a trapped spouse leaves.

The evidence resulting from these decisions is irrefutable. Children deprived of a father are far more likely to be involved in criminal activity than those in a two-parent household. Statistics reveal fatherless children to be:

1. 72% of all teenage murderers.
2. 60% of rapists.
3. 70% of kids incarcerated.
4. Twice as likely to quit school.
5. 11 times more likely to be violent.
6. 3 of 4 teen suicides.
7. 80% of the adolescents in psychiatric hospitals.
8. 90% of runaways.

Sources: National Fatherhood Initiative (U.S.A.), US Bureau of Census (U.S.A.), FBI (U.S.A.)

These are kids rebelling against a world they feel doesn't care about them. They feel they weren't good enough to stick around for, when in fact, they were not the cause of their father's abandonment—aimlessness, panic or fraud was—but by then it is too late. I certainly don't excuse men who use women, but predatory men hurt *feelings*, while predatory women forever alter human lives. To secure financial support, the more callous women can effectively vilify the father in the child's eyes and make it almost impossible for him to see his children, and the law isn't helping:

"Father-deprivation is a serious form of child abuse that is institutionalized and entrenched within our legal system. Powerful sexist people have a vested interest in diminishing the role of men, especially their role as fathers. Research proves that children thrive with the active and meaningful participation of both biological parents, and is true for post-divorce families."

– *"Child Custody or Child Abuse"*, Victoria Times-Colonist, Jan 8, 1998

"While the law allows women to turn casual sex into cash flow sex, Penelope Leach, in her book Children First, poses an essential question: "Why is it socially reprehensible for a man to

leave a baby fatherless, but courageous, even admirable, for a woman to have a baby whom she knows will be so?"
—Amy Alkon

To foster this, a woman is given a clear legal pattern for transgression upon a man. A man must finance the endeavor, regardless of what a woman does to conceive. The legal and *moral r*esponse to securing values through fraud in any other realm is time and restitution, but in this case, the penalties are reserved for the victim. Men are legally defenseless; it is the most convenient way to steal the life-force of another.

Our own President has said, *"The real problem is unwed mothers"*, yet the government honors their pattern. As sound family is the foundation of society, its violation is a foundational weakness for the country. The law cannot encourage illegitimate children—it must break the pattern. Nine times out of ten, if she knew she couldn't get away with it, it would never happen. If welfare seekers could get no more money after two children, they would get fixed after two. *"There is nothing as heart-wrenching as a hungry child?"* Well, it is nothing compared to the collapse of a nation by internal corruption. Overpopulation, rent-control slums, inner-city crime and societal breakdown... the whole problem and all the devastation it spawns would be reduced back to 2-5% of total births, were it not honored by law.

In the meantime, a useful reminder for us all is that **Sex leads to babies!** Before you do it, ask yourself, "Would

I want a child with this person?" if the answer is no, go home!

Relationships and parenting are too important to be indulged in casually. Kids need *both* mom and dad for their best chance to turn out well, and a man has a right to wait for the conditions he finds conducive to his being a good mate and father. Children must be a product of love, trust, mutual respect, and sound life progression—not of fraud, contempt, and aimlessness. This is the greatest moral obligation of women, and the route to their highest pride as a patriot. You have to *know* that by your actions, you will build a strong family, which in turn builds a stronger America. Face it bravely: *only have children with a man who openly wants children with you.* Until this glaring vulnerability is corrected, the future of our country will be in jeopardy. The world needs to see it clearly: motherhood is *only* beautiful with the father's consent. Waiting for the right time, our future children will be given much more spiritually than what a drained, unhappy parent could share.

Divorce and Community Property

The concept of *community property* is rooted in Communism. To consider a two million dollar estate to be half-owned by an unemployed spouse with no means—male or female—is ludicrous. There is no rational separation between property and the effort put forth to acquire it. The law should not permit one spouse to victimize another, but elements of our own evasion often gets us into situations our most honest selves would avoid. Both partners should be able to say "I'm marrying you for *you*, not for your property," signing an enforceable document to that effect. Otherwise, watch out! The pursuit of security is a strong motivation for the fear-driven. It precedes love, attraction, and mutual goals: all that justifies a sound marriage.

Institutionalized Indigence

We cringe at the thought of helping the deadbeats in our own families—they are black holes in whom all investment is squandered—but we do it as a nation through welfare, subsidies, and social security. All are the slavery of a faceless victim. Combining a tin cup with a gun, these programs oppose the life-pattern of capitalist action in favor of *death*-patterns—without intellectual engagement, self-generation, or continuing value, dealing only with the physical matter of consumption. The bleeding hearts only appear that way: the blood is ours.

Welfare

Some percentage of mankind is comfortable in squalor and will never aspire, but our government is responsible for *greatly expanding* our slums through welfare. If people never intend to work and are permitted to receive a poverty level allotment, they must then seek housing suitable to their aim. They look for the lowest rent or none at all, and let it go to hell. It isn't pretty, but it's free. They learn to stretch that allotment by paying for every third month's rent, being evicted every quarter. If welfare pays for seven kids, they have seven before considering birth control, as more kids would be *their* expense. Hence, smart money management combined with absolutely no integrity provides a complete lifestyle. The result is a geometrically expanding plethora of cannibal voters versus the two-child average for a moral, self-supporting family, who vote for the biggest liar while devouring their cities in ruins and decay.

The bad news is, we the productive, cannot escape it. We laughingly try to administer their affairs and hold them accountable to our system, ignoring the implications of their intellectual chaos, which makes sound civil conduct impossible. Rampant ignorance, crime, and bad taste will overwhelm us by sheer numbers, tainting everything in its path with the foul rot of neglect. Should we really give the world away to a segment of the population that has no moral values, no education, no class, and won't lift a finger to sustain their own lives?

Not to mention our health risk from the loafers at the other end of the spectrum, the thieving rich. For centuries, Malthus has had them targeting the "useless eaters" for annihilation worldwide. With such a focused approach easily detected in the US, the way chosen has been general exposure to contaminants and suppression of cures, expecting the weakest in body and mind to expire first. In this scenario, we are all victims of this diabolical lottery.

Poverty and graft are immoral patterns, which welfare breeds and sanctions. It is not further consumption its recipients need to practice—they have that down—but the pattern of living cognition itself. Welfare entitlements are an anchor, which will drag the country into the abyss if permitted to continue. Frankly, it's hard to imagine winning either way: cut them off and they will be robbing our homes while we work; kidnapping our children for ransom; mugging us in the street. Life would become a constant peril for the middle class. With jails overloaded, FEMA would get to use their Nazi camps after all. Such would be the new civil war—not between the haves and the have-not's, but between the *wills* and the *will-not's*.

If people don't need you, you *should* be afraid. Personally, I'd rather face the music than continue to pay them to do nothing. I say, sink or swim, like I had to when I joined the adult world at 18. All such government programs should end. They would quickly be replaced by local missions for those who *truly* need help. If welfare's recipients *have to* find honorable sources to survive (given survival is their intent), they will. The rest are doomed.

Social Security

Social Security was a system designed and adopted by the USSR in the 1920's—a plan to steal the wealth of the nation under the guise of caring for them—which was modified and adopted by the United States in 1935 as a moronic answer to the Great Depression. Since then, money is allotted, money gets stolen. Money is borrowed, money is mismanaged. The New Deal with all its new rights was pure Socialism—and unconstitutional by the way—the spectacle of an oaf generously distributing money he didn't earn. No matter what mindless ideal a politician pursues, as soon as you are parted from your money, it is gone. If you think it is logical or safe to have faith in the government and then look the other way, just ask any German.

At a minimum, this should be your account at your bank, managed by you but limited to safe instruments, to be drawn on due to specific life requirements—be it medical or financial crisis, and ultimately, retirement.

Subsidies

The forced sanction of a product is just artificial demand: an indication that the product shouldn't exist. We stockpile milk to help dairy farmers because it is a product that isn't selling. We push it as a health benefit when next to fluoride, cheese and milk are the worst things we put in our bodies. "Got cancer?" Set those cows free and grow some vegetables.

A person can't even touch pure fluoride—*they would die*, but it is difficult to dispose of industrial waste, so it is easier for corporations if you just eat it. How about following up that fluoride treatment with a swig of motor oil?

Environmentalism

Why is their focus not on the brilliant sky and our productive harmony under it, but on the small column of smoke coming from a ship's engine? Why do they look, not at the limitless countryside, but at the small rectangle advertising products of free trade along the highways which they also hate? Civilization cannot exist harvesting what grows in the wild without our control. A handful of men might be able to survive running through forests, eating berries, building huts from dead branches—but not an industrial society.

The most extreme claim we must not disturb a blade of grass. To tread is wrong in itself; for Man to live is an affront to all that which exists in harmony, *only* without us. Yet as productive men, we tie our lives to the very fabric of nature, as there are only two ways to live—off the land, or off of each other. By intellectual default, they promote this last. Speaking to the extreme environmentalists, "Let's grant your wish hypothetically, and let you knock down all the smoke stacks. Running errands, you go to the grocery store and stare in horror at the empty shelves. You planned to hit many more stores, but passing a number of closed gas stations, you get an ominous feeling and decide to conserve what's in your tank. Getting the mail at home, you have an emergency tax bill to help cover all the unemployed you've just thrown out of work. Your boss calls to say that a major supplier's factory has been mysteriously shut down, and your products can no longer be made—*you're* out of work too. No more paychecks and no more food, but what do you need them for? It's a beautiful day. You have a blissful, pollution-free world to gaze at while you die."

All elements of an idea must be known in order to maintain its result properly, be it a business, an agricultural supply-line or a philosophy. There is no way to scale back intelligence and still benefit from what it produces. No expropriation is successful long-term, when the tops are cut down to force solutions to questions the environmentalists have no civil answer for, and no tolerance or mental discipline to reach. Do we see great technological advances out of the Roman Catholic Church? Out of Greenpeace? Out of Ralph Nader? No; only criticism, threats, and demands. They operate from a fixed mind, so they imagine all values to be fixed as well. They see a fixed amount of oil on the planet and a fixed amount of food. They determine that there is only so much to go around and grant no consideration for Man's continuous efficiencies, which extrapolate the preservation, bounty, and longevity of raw materials. No faith is placed in Man's mind, because those who focus on this never-ending stream of panicked contrivances have negated theirs. Ultimately, the advances to lessen our environmental impact will most likely come from the same disciplined thinkers who gave us automobiles, computers, and running water.

To the environmentalist's credit, some have uncovered instances of abuse that are truly deplorable. I have watched footage of Japanese fishing boats cutting fins off sharks and dumping the bodies (exploiting the high profit "shark-fin soup" market), leaving them to endure a horrible death. As a supporter of free enterprise, a sinking feeling had to ask, *"Is this what I represent?"* The answer is no. Such waste and inefficiency would be clobbered in a laissez-faire economy where businesses pay for their raw materials. But they get the fish for nothing—incurring no cost or penalty above honest fishing vessels for wasting their stock. They wouldn't be so wasteful with ponds they own. If I was in a ship close by, I wouldn't think twice about putting a torpedo through their hull. Oops! Survival of the fittest... We are best served as capitalists to remain aware of the motives behind what is done in our name. Man's rights do not include piracy or rape. My respect for *all* life disallows supporting such heartbreaking, inhumane wastefulness.

An integrated path that respects human life must be formed, and awareness of that is spreading. Civilization must be maintained, and *of course* we must be responsible for our actions—maximizing utilization of the products we draw from the ground or the water—which is simply good business sense. Mankind is *not* in a struggle opposed to nature. One doesn't have to go—it isn't *either/or* anymore. Listen to the Discovery Channel and you will see their pitches for nature beginning to show respect for industry—which is respect for human life—bringing environmentalism around to reason *finally*, and I'm glad to support this frame of mind.

Freeing Energy: Alternatives to Oil and Gas

Fossil fuel prices fluctuate; sometimes it is in our favor, other times, it brings us to our knees. We can't forget about it when times are good; we have to keep pushing ahead to replace them and remove our dependence on unstable nations. (In fact, this whole book is about energy independence; not just for America, but for individuals, as proper moral awareness is the foundation of a sovereign being, and a sovereign being is master of his or her own energy.) We must never let those who would bind us in moral confusion steal our living energy; just as we must never again let foreign oil—as OPEC did in the 1970's—hold our country for ransom.

Alternative, viable technologies have existed for over a century, yet have been repressed to assure oil remains a principle commodity. Even motors that run on *pressurized air* exist today in various stages of development. Battery and hybrid technologies are increasing in range and are going mainstream. Wind and tidal power generators are becoming more effective and less obtrusive as well. Despite the automotive trauma in Detroit, it is an exciting time for transportation designers of all kinds. This industry is spreading over the continent, lighting a fire in young minds and exciting new ideas from unexpected sources, creating more jobs and attracting more investors as they awaken to understand that this drive will shape America and perhaps the world for the next thousand years.

The independence of energy production—right down to where individuals can earn money and contribute to the grid on an exercise bike—will be the foundation of a new freedom. It can be a hedge against unemployment and a protection against those seeking to weaken us: an effective check against unjust abuses afforded those of public or private power. As the U.S. Constitution institutes governments among men, energy independence could result in the greatest distribution of wealth and security this country has ever seen.

Runaway Judgments

I recall hearing about a lung cancer case where a jury awarded something like *$75 billion dollars* to a woman who claimed she didn't know smoking was bad for her. This was hailed in the media as *"sending a message to the tobacco companies that we aren't going to take it anymore."* Say fifty thousand people are employed in that industry, all whose financial fate rests on the outcome. In that judgment, we take the working capital that represents the living energy of *fifty thousand people* and perhaps one hundred years of successful business inertia, and dump it on one moron who has done nothing more than get sick by her own stupidity, then was begged to sue by some parasite lawyer stalking the emphysema ward.

If a decision explodes to an improper magnitude, it doesn't help the country. They claim that life is priceless—a sentiment most would agree with—but try to actualize it by inflicting judgments so large that they wipe out fifty thousand lives to restore one. If ten percent of one's living power is lost by product failure, then ten percent is recompense. For the sake of economic stability, a cap must be placed on all judgments which respect the *true* loss—a range determined by the court for the jury to decide *within*.

Judicial Transparency

More and more often in America vicious crimes are perpetrated, both victims and alleged murderers are killed, and the authorities are free to make up whatever story they like. The public smells the possibility of an outright fabrication, weakening our trust of government. For this reason, there should be a legal obligation to try all high profile cases regardless of who is alive or dead to testify. There should be full discovery: full access to all evidence on both sides to establish a complete historical record. Judges or deciding bodies should be publically chosen and qualified for impartiality, subject to overrule by citizen panels, and face serious penalties for obstructing the process or abusing their positions.

Antitrust and Centralized Control

Antitrust legislation permits the government to bring charges against any business pricing higher, lower, or equal to their competition. Are eyebrows appropriately raised? Pricing higher is considered *gouging*. Pricing lower is considered *dumping*. Pricing the same is considered *collusion*. As all business activity falls into one of these categories, there is no innocence to declare other than sanity, and the surest protection for a business is simply never to be successful. The most recent case that hit home for me was the antitrust suit against Microsoft. It is embarrassing that a man as capable as Bill Gates has to sit there and listen to "Experts" (men with dismal track records by comparison) theorize about how his business *could* be run—and they expect him to risk his own money on *their* viewpoint? It was pointless anyway: with the speed of technology, Washington didn't prove as effective a monopolistic deterrent as the open source programming of Linux.

How many class action suits resulting in fifty-seven cents per customer across the nation (if they care to fill out the paperwork and waste a stamp) are going to be fought before officials realize antitrust has mutated into a parasitical business tax benefiting only law firms? They restrain trade *themselves* and at their worst, commit the moral horror of jailing executives for nothing more than providing the public with products they want in a voluntary market. I bought a pair of shoes once and started receiving legal documents stating the progress and terms of an antitrust suit against their maker. The law firm made millions off the case, making it well worth their while, but I don't think my human rights were violated in paying slightly more for a pair of shoes.

Morally, this legislation has strayed. Rather than protecting consumers from different forms of hegemony, it offers the legal profession a steady means of graft and fails to address the true social impacts of corporate malfeasance upon the nation. As executives of large companies move easily between private and public positions, perhaps a more direct link should be established between antitrust legislation and the American Bill of Rights, to specifically monitor any organization's encroachment upon our civil liberties. No fields suffer such glaring encroachments today as banking, healthcare, farming, and media. Our fundamental rights have been stripped by the weight of new laws driven by fear, indicating the need for a *"Citizens First"* legal guideline to counter this threat.

"Economies of scale" lower costs and make more and better products available for all, but this concept deserves great and careful scrutiny when brought into the realm of government and monopolies. Cultivation and refinement are often the moral inverse of consolidation and control. Governments are instituted among men to *avoid* consolidated power, which always turns corrupt by the Fear-driven in pursuit of irrational self-preservation and a false image.

Lobbies

The Fear-driven wish to force their betters to provide what nature cannot give them: guarantees. Irrational lobbies are the con man's equivalent of the Self-made's patent, copyright, and trademark. In such forms as subsidies and charters, they attempt to survive by transferring the burden of their instabilities to the rest of us. The State is just a group of men with one critical difference—the capacity to legislate—which means the right to initiate the use of force against others. When violence is allowed in industry, *pull* becomes the currency—the hottest commodity—and the easiest to lose control of.

The power to grant monopolies, bar competition, and dictate regulations—rational or not—forces businessmen into a struggle for legal advantages. Laws go to protect the highest bidder and leave our society's moral efficiency for dead until enough of a public uproar is made. It is not the fault of businessmen per se; while some use political subversion to gain advantages, the rest must pay representatives to protect themselves *from* it, minimizing where they would prefer to invest—in scientific and commercial advancements. Such a power drives the good men out, then drives the very good out of those who remain.

If you wonder why nothing changes, it is because like-minded politicians make a business of it. Just as you choose raw materials for the composition of your products, *your life and production* is the value behind any deal they make. If a new check were added to the process, giving the people a direct vote on issues critical to them through the internet, the number of people corrupt men would have to bribe would be unlimited, and therefore impossible. Technology makes this system reform possible, and outrageous conduct in Washington makes it essential. Such a website network would limit the power of our representatives to take advantage as well. It should disclose all lobbies involved and have each senator provide details and their own viewpoints so their constituents can make well-informed decisions.

Endless Internal Revenue

In today's world, you would be hard pressed to find anyone expecting to see the day when income taxes are abolished. Barely anyone would entertain the serious possibility of ridding ourselves of it, even though our government already collects enough income from other sources to fund its justifiable expenses without income tax.

If you hand over five hundred dollars per week through taxes, do you think you are getting five hundred dollars' worth of assistance in living your life? Do you think you could do better with the money than they have? Out of a year, we pay almost six months of taxes; *six months* of working with no right to keep the results of our effort; and for what end?

A society is greatly weakened by over-taxation. History shows that a nation's overrun and collapse is often due to corruptly incurred debt via the pawned-off responsibility for its recompense—pushed on those who have no say. The tax base is just the checkbook of the country, and what it pays for is to be decided by us. We need a *"line item veto"* for the people of the United States to exercise on April 15th. This should be accounting day for the government, listing expenses so that the people can cross out what they no longer wish to fund. Whatever lacks mass support or cannot be defended with clear reasoning should be dropped, and the savings returned to the people.

Term Limits

We have all heard of catastrophic government waste, but often it isn't premeditated; many politicians have no inkling of sound living patterns. They believe government is all powerful and can provide anything they ask, like a rich kid who has everything done for him. Those entering politics straight out of college don't even know *how* to live and aren't going to make sensible decisions.

For the reason of core competence, we need to add career politicians to the endangered species list. With term limits for *all* elected posts—*none* being longer than the chief executive—we can better guarantee that politicians will have spent at least a part of their lives earning a living; and then efficient, responsible action will be second nature to them.

Campaign Finance Reform

A grotesque distortion of justice was perpetrated in the U.S. Supreme Court's *Citizens United* ruling, equating a corporation with an individual. It claimed that any limits on political advertising were unconstitutional as this would bar free speech. The problem is that rarely are corporations—those able to invest large sums for political aims—made up of 100% Americans. Most large companies have parent companies, subsidiaries, plants, sales offices, and storefronts all over the world, and a mix of employees and executives who come from vastly different backgrounds. The First Amendment is an American statute that applies solely to American individuals and groups, voting for American political offices.

We would not let Russians come here and take to the streets with communist propaganda. We would not invoke the First Amendment in defense of a foreign nation taking control of our media. The Constitution is for American citizens and their voluntary associations only, and the smallest common denominator is the individual. *"One man, one vote"* implies a fair balance: that one man's influence over the outcome is the same as any other man's. The corrupt influence of concentrated wealth is something Democracy thrives without.

If a company is making $50 billion a year and a political race—federal, state, or local—that effects their interests typically costs $5 million, why wouldn't they try to buy a positive result? For this reason, elections should be publically funded as an essential attribute of the democratic machinery, removing the advantage of those seeking to buy the political process.

Free Elections

"The people who cast the votes decide nothing. The people who count the votes decide everything." —Joseph Stalin

Voting shenanigans have been a part of the political process since voting was invented. After LBJ won his Senate race in 1948, it was found that Box 13, the deciding ballot box, was stuffed with votes from the local cemetery. This was discovered because the deceased voters seemed to have staggered in in alphabetical order.

History records an impressive stream of deceitful techniques to discourage, repress, and bar individuals from voting, from intimidation and harassment, to the destruction of genuine ballots and creation of fakes, to confusing and delaying voters. The more blatant, violent, and easily traced tactics could be retired however, with the invention of the voting machine.

Electronic voting machines have been shown on live television to be easily hacked, and over the years the makers have been sued for fraud, bribery, and improper political affiliations. It should be obvious that once an electronic vote is cast with no paper trail, all objectivity is lost.

We should not be pursuing maximum efficiency in our most basic democratic processes when the result could so easily undermine the will of the people. Paper records are not prone to malfunction or manipulation, and are easily recounted. As a country, we should return to paper ballots marked in permanent ink, counted publically by local representatives with a video record. If issues arise, they should be locally litigated with no federal interference of any kind. Pressing the voter's thumb on an inkpad whose stain won't fade for at least 24 hours will assure an individual only votes once. We must restore confidence in this process for our union to remain strong.

Politics and Internal Corruption

In a perfect world, we can trust our leaders. Those running the government should be as fully accountable as the citizens they serve; they shouldn't also be tied to huge corporations privately benefiting from every policy decision. We haven't reached a perfect world because many of those now in power *don't want it*. Our laws and foreign policies should be geared to protect our country and honor personal freedoms everywhere; not to confiscate or pillage America or foreign lands.

Politicians can get so corrupt that all of their decisions begin to affect us directly. When those with ties to military or infrastructure contractors get into office, questionable events often occur that raise tensions in the world, resulting in misery for the citizens and massive profits for the companies they represent (for example, Johnson/Bell Helicopter and more recently, Bush/Carlyle Group/Bin-Laden Group). Our richest citizens and political families aren't supposed to get rich by systematically ripping off the rest. Mass deception is not forgivable. Life-taking actions are *not* forgivable. Incivility is not forgivable. By morally empowering all men, *we will take from them this power.*

Sidestepping your consciousness allows immoral people endless opportunities to hide their motivations. Clean motives have nothing to worry about; they *enjoy* an audience. Deadly motives loath awareness, and in self-defense, therefore demand it. We must require full disclosure to follow and record everything politicians do. This includes full financial disclosure keeping all accounts public, including a regular means test for personal acquisitions.

This isn't a land we are going to surrender to corrupt politicians or filthy artists or welfare frauds. *This is American soil.* If you love it, you've got to fight for it. We must dissolve political corruption and moral disunity *inside* America before we can be truly effective solving problems *outside.* We must know for certain what the politicians are doing in our name, and bring to this world the honor that every child expects to encounter in adulthood.

Freeing Our Money

"If the American people ever allow private banks to control the issue of their currency, first by inflation, then by deflation, the banks...will deprive the people of all property until their children wake-up homeless on the continent their fathers conquered."
—Thomas Jefferson, 1809

From earliest recorded history, mankind has made a stair-step progression in everything but finance. Our technology and standard of living runs a race with currency control, a facet that unless we take command of, we will eventually lose to. What is startling is how early America's money troubles began:

"The Colonies would gladly have borne the little tax on tea and other matters had it not been the poverty caused by the bad influence of the English bankers on the Parliament, which has caused in the Colonies hatred of England and the Revolutionary War." —Benjamin Franklin

In the Declaration of the Causes and Necessity of Taking Up Arms of July 6, 1775, John Hancock wrote: *"They [the British] have undertaken to give and grant our money without our consent, though we have ever exercised an exclusive right to dispose of our own property."*

It wasn't long after our victory that we faced another financial crisis, fought by President Andrew Jackson. He considered an American central bank to be a massive threat to the safety of the republic, as *"it represented a fantastic centralization of economic and political power under private control. It was a "monopoly" with special privileges, and yet it was not subject to presidential, congressional, or popular regulation."* —Robert V. Remini (Jackson biographer). Jackson ultimately destroyed the bank and was the only President in history to pay off our national debt. A generation later, a new President deplored their influence as well:

"I have two great enemies, the southern army in front of me and the financial institutions in the rear. Of the two, the one in the rear is the greatest enemy. The money power preys upon the nation in times of peace, and conspires against it in times of adversity." —Abraham Lincoln

Unable to secure affordable funds for the war, Lincoln's counsel suggested he print his own interest-free currency to pay Union troops with—the origin of Greenbacks. The success of the plan prompted Lincoln to exclaim, *"The privilege of creating and issuing the money is not only the supreme prerogative of Government, but it is the Government's greatest creative opportunity. By the adoption of these principles...the taxpayers will be saved immense sums of interest...Money will cease to be master and become the servant of humanity."*

The London Times (in 1865) responded with startling honesty: "If this mischievous financial policy, which has its origin in the American Republic, shall become permanent, then that government will furnish its own money without cost! It will pay off its debts and be without debt. It will have all the money necessary to carry on its commerce. It will become prosperous without precedent in the history of the world. The brains and the wealth of all countries will go to America. That government must be destroyed or it will destroy every monarchy on the globe!"

In his travels before the assassination of Lincoln, John Wilkes Booth gathered financial support in the drawing rooms of European bankers. Every President to scrutinize currency control has had an attempt made on his life, including Andrew Jackson, John F. Kennedy, and Ronald Reagan. Congressional records documented a little-known plot to overthrow Franklin D. Roosevelt for reversing the banker's constriction of capital (which caused the Great Depression). Within the records, the bankers admitted their complete control over the media (even then) as an essential ingredient. Those who have spoken out have done so at great personal risk:

"Whosoever controls the volume of money in any country is absolute master of all industry and commerce... And when you realize that the entire system is very easily controlled, one way or another, by a few powerful men at the top, you will not have to be told how periods of inflation and depression originate."

—President James Garfield, June of 1881.

He was assassinated two weeks later.

Modern Economic Control

The Federal Reserve controls the money supply in three ways: 1) Selling or buying U.S. government bonds from the government or in the bond market. To *sell* bonds is to contract the currency, decreasing the supply of money. To *buy* bonds is to inflate the currency, increasing the quantity of money. 2) Raising or lowering bank reserve requirements. To raise reserve requirements is a *tightening* that decreases the money supply, making money harder to obtain. To lower reserve requirements is a *loosening* that increases the money supply and makes loans easier to obtain. 3) Changing the discount rate—the rate that banks borrow money created by the Fed to lend to the public.

These elements are popularly considered essential to control market dynamics, but are little more than layers of coercive control. Their justification was that with this power, depressions could be scientifically prevented. The problem, as congressman Charles A. Lindberg retorted, was that, *"From now on, depressions will be scientifically created."*

"To cause high prices, all the Federal Reserve Board will do, will be to lower the rediscount rate...producing an expansion of credit and a rising stock market, then when...businessmen are used to

those conditions, it can check prosperity in mid-career by arbitrarily raising the rate of interest.

It can cause the pendulum of a rising and falling market to swing gently back and forth by slight changes in the discount rate, or cause violent fluctuations by a greater rate variation, and in either case it will possess inside information as to financial conditions and advance knowledge of the coming change, either up or down.

This is the strangest, most dangerous advantage ever placed in the hands of the special privilege class by any government that ever existed. The system is private, conducted for the sole purpose of obtaining the greatest possible profits from the use of other people's money. They know in advance when to create panics to their advantage. They also know when to stop panic. Inflation and deflation work equally well for them when they control finance."

—Charles A. Lindberg (R-MN)

The Illegitimacy of Bonds

All of our money is considered *borrowed* money (yielding interest), even though it isn't. The currency is a *fresh* creation, backed by the good faith of the American population. This is how money is created by the Fed: 1) The Federal Open Market Committee (FOMC) approves the purchase of U.S. bonds, which are simply a promise to pay. 2) The bonds are "purchased" by the Fed. 3) The Fed pays for the bonds with electronic credits added to the bond seller's bank, but these credits are based on nothing—they are created with the flick of a pen! 4) The bank uses the deposits as reserves, and can loan out up to *ten times* the amount of the reserves to new borrowers—all at interest. We see our mortgage interest at perhaps ten percent, but at this reserve ratio, the bank can make *one-hundred percent* on the money.

This method of monetary creation is fundamentally unsound. The creation of a bond must be based on an existing financial instrument. The currency must *precede* the bond and not be created *by* the bond, as to retire the bond is to destroy the currency. But the Fed issues currency for bonds as if they're lending, because lending produces interest.

"If our nation can issue a dollar bond it can issue a dollar bill. The element that makes the bond good makes the bill good, also. The difference between the bond and the bill is that the bond lets the money brokers collect twice the amount of the bond and an additional 20 percent, whereas the currency pays nobody but those who directly contribute in some useful way. It is absurd to say that our country can issue $30 million in bonds and not $30 million in currency. Both are promises to pay, but one promise fattens the usurer and the other, helps the people."

—Thomas Edison, 1921

Sound Money and Sound Banking

In a mortal struggle for power, currency control has changed hands from public to private *eight times* since our country's inception. The conflict lies at the base of our right of property, and the desire of the corrupt elite to rob us of it. The safe store of value sought by Man is not to be found in commodities such as gold or silver. It is found in human productivity, that part of a man's life that is spent sustaining his existence. This is an inexhaustible and incorruptible source of wealth—replenished and consumed again, every single day. The question to ask the Federal Reserve is, "What moral action have *you* taken to bring this money into existence?"

Our monetary system was the first terrorist attack on the United States. Every great evil the corrupt rich have been able to perpetrate since, stems from it. It is time to end this threat; the future of the civilized world depends on it. We must take away their power to create money with no balancing creation of value. We must remove their power to make money scarce or plenty. We must stop paying interest on money we never borrowed in the first place. No more secret meetings. No subversive political influence. No more *means* to engineer depressions.

"I believe that banking institutions are more dangerous to our liberties than standing armies...The issuing power should be taken from the banks and restored to the people, to whom it properly belongs." —Thomas Jefferson, 1809

Imagine waiting at a checkout, watching a man who charged up a credit card until it gets declined, then another, then another. You see him with a whole stack, frustratingly trying to secure his purchase and you know he is on the road to doom. We pity such predicaments. Think of your own sensible spending habits and careful budgeting. Now imagine someone like him taking *your* credit cards and doing this, leaving you to pay it all back. *That* is Quantitative Easing.

We cannot *spur* an aging population to spend through monetary stimulus; not when the mass of our citizens are preparing for retirement. Under such circumstances, a long-term economic contraction is appropriate and predictable. Charging up our credit cards and getting all other countries to do the same just spells worldwide bankruptcy, weakened sovereignty, and will result in an attempt to dissolve our more perfect union in favor of one despotic world government.

Capitalism is not impervious to the devastation of an ill-conceived monetary system. When foundations are laid poorly, all that is built on them is at risk of collapse. To solve the problem, all debt-based currencies worldwide must be abolished. We can start here by replacing Federal Reserve notes with debt-free U.S. Treasury notes, resulting in an immediate savings of $360 billion plus per year. Our income tax burden would be cut in half with no loss of government services. The concept of fractional reserve banking must be abolished as well. No one gets to generate interest on money they never earned to begin with. No central interest rate controls. No inflation booms and contraction busts. By rebuilding our system on full reserve banking, every girder is real. All Americans should profit by the fairness of the design.

No Presidential platform is worthwhile today unless it addresses currency reform, assuring transparency, accountability, and guarding against unwarranted political influence. Never again should we let private banks control and issue our money, thereby permitting a secret government to rise, challenge, and undermine the morally sanctioned government agreed upon by all.

Freeing Our Time *and* Money

In America, 30-year home mortgages are the norm. At the peak of the housing bubble, 40 and 50-year loans were cropping up. At Japan's peak, homeowners began taking on 100 year mortgages; a debt which would then be passed down within their families. Amortizing so slowly, homeowners gather very little equity while the majority of the payment goes toward interest. With a 30-year loan, you would pay two to three times the price of your house to the bank. With a 50-year loan, it would be three to four times the price of your house, and just for the joy of disbelief, a 100-year loan would cost you four to *nine times* the price of your house. Just to borrow money the central bank created out of thin air anyway.

30 Year $100,000 Loan @ 5%: Total Paid: $193,256
30 Year $100,000 Loan @ 10%: Total Paid: $315,926

50 Year $100,000 Loan @ 5%: Total Paid: $272,483
50 Year $100,000 Loan @ 10%: Total Paid: $503,463

100 Year $100,000 Loan @ 5%: Total Paid: $403,524
100 Year $100,000 Loan @ 10%: Total Paid: $907,428

The uninitiated might say, *"Wow, how generous of the bank to take a chance on me"* without recognizing they have become a debt slave. It is no wonder that the original meaning of *"mortgage"* is *"death pledge."* It would be much more generous for the bank to shield you from all that interest so that you could pay the loan down quickly. Imagine what life would look like if this were so. As a culture, buying, affording, and paying off a house would not be a 30 year-to-lifetime burden, but a 5-7 year plan. You could then spend the rest of your time and money on your kids, for travel, to start a business, to conduct research, for retirement, or whatever you could dream up; there would be no limits. You could work 24 hours a week instead of 40 or 50. Three days on, four days off. You could do what you wanted, not what you *had* to, *for life*. Think of how you could spend your time if you didn't have to work thirty years to afford a mortgage and maintain an expensive lifestyle: dwell on that question for a while. Pay corrupt bankers or pay yourself: *it's up to you*, so let's explore how.

Interest Shield

It is important to study other cultures, as often you will find our nation's evils exposing themselves by contrast. From land to land, corruption takes different forms, as does honor. In Australia for example, the typical home mortgage is for 5-7 years. It is amortized for 30 years to establish a payment, but the loan is given in two parts. For a $100,000 loan, the borrower is given a $90,000 mortgage and a revolving $10,000 home equity line, with the agreement that the borrower deposit his or her income checks onto the home equity line for the life of the mortgage. Bills are paid throughout the month out of this account as with a normal checking account, but instead of your money sitting idle in a non-interest bearing account, it is working to shield you from the hideous interest accumulating on the mortgage.

Say you net $5,000 per month. That means half your home equity line will bear no interest, and if you don't spend everything you make, say $500-1,000 stays in the account each month, that $10,000 loan will be repaid in a year. What do you do then? Transfer another $10,000 from the equity line onto the main mortgage. Now you owe about $80,000 and $10,000. In five to seven cycles of this process, your home will be paid off.

Every homeowner and prospective homeowner in America deserves to know about this. You can find mortgage amortization charts for accelerated pay down at one or all of my sites: MoralArmor.com, EthicsReloaded.com, or CareandFeedingofFreedom.com. This is the biggest middle finger I can think of that we can give to the corrupt rich and their debt-money banking system. The quicker we become debt free, the less vulnerable we are to the financial calamities imposed on us by those looking to centralize all power, feed off of us, and ultimately determine our fate.

Chapter Nine

Countering America's Opposition

I am honored to recognize the kind of friends America has, and equally, the kind of enemies she has. Contemplating a man like Benjamin Franklin, you have to ask, "Who could justify *not* liking him?" If you encountered a person who didn't like someone so honest and fair, intelligent and sincere, patient and responsible, it is a good indicator you have found someone who is *none* of those things. If you are a good person, *that's* the kind of enemy you want.

It is like that with America's enemies; bad vibes abound on a very personal level. Our friends are just the opposite; positive and wholesome on a very personal level. In any conflict, I'm proud to be on the side of what has always been called "the Allied Powers." Still, I hope one day we see our enemies awaken to a new perspective that aligns us all in peace. But until then...

Extremists

"When a man's life has no value, sometimes death has its price."
—Fistful of Dollars

Religion is partially responsible for terrorism, and not just one faith in particular. Those teaching, *"independence is evil"*, shouldn't be surprised when kids join gangs. Violating cognition is an act of Spirit Murder, and in an unstable environment, it won't be long before it is extrapolated into physical murder. When a consciousness rapidly degenerates, it builds towards an explosion. What happens when children are taught to defy consciousness right from the beginning? Internal anarchy quickly results in external anarchy. They grow confident in being rude and threatening to their parents, but are lost and uncertain when they step outside. By an extension of the same dogma, that negativity is led by a more seasoned force to its ultimate end, and they draw him to his death like a poodle on a string.

Religious fanaticism perpetuates the tragic melding of cognition with interaction, which leads terrorist minions to their deaths. Fanaticism as well justifies confiscation, sacrifice and destruction for *"a good cause,"* which for a morality where anything goes and no one is to blame, means *any cause they choose.* The advantage they take stems from and feeds on cognitive limitations, and with every dogmatic claim violating the true pattern, terrorist theory is implicitly supported by every mother and grandmother preaching the gospel. Furnish their people with a modern city, and their primitive religious premises would turn it right back into shambles.

A country's citizens would never need to leave their homeland and flee to safe havens if it were not so; if it were not for their non-objective, unrealistically substantiated, unaccountable religious doctrines. Instead of striving for an envisioned future glory, they shoot their citizens in the back while they try to escape the horror, where the trigger is first pulled on rationality—their own cognitive accountability. We hear them say *"You have to be willing to sacrifice yourself for the greater good,"* or, *"We cannot see His whole plan,"* and end up fighting over what it is and what it isn't, and who has the authority to say so; but no one can step outside the context of existence itself to make *existential* connections. The only alternative to rationality, is violence.

We must grow to the stature of accepting *our own* determinations of moral substance, and that requires a logical standard. Unless we accept that our senses *are* valid, we invite and *justify* this kind of aggression. An appeased aggressor just becomes more aggressive.

Zealots

From outer space, you can see that the Edison's of mankind light up the world, whereas those of the lowest intellect, prone to anarchy such as mercenaries and terrorists, just leave little splat marks. Accomplishments determine a man's stature, and destruction only subtracts from it. Where are the great buildings and societies as a result of their philosophy? Ideology is fought not with bombs, but with ideology. Why can't they fight us ideologically? Because theirs is worthless. Was Jesus running around slaughtering his opposition, or was his ministry and following peaceful and voluntary? Jesus wasn't a murdering, threatening Neanderthal. Did the prophets interpret religion so they could rape and kill freely? Did Moses? Who are the extremist's *real* idols then? Who have the terrorists and zealots *really* patterned their lives after? That is right, the prophet's brutal, scavenging enemies. Violence is a confession of cowardice—of intellectual impotence. Listen to their foolish incoherent explanations they hope no one will question. Their veil of dogmatic justification is so thin that they typically have to die or kill their audience before the truth is named—by others or within their own minds. One more dead is one less to convince, or to admit the truth to of what it is they are doing.

There is no room for zealots in morality. There are no wife-beating, child-molesting, peer and student-threatening, red-faced, fist-shaking convincing tactics that are EVER utilized by rational beings. Such people aren't even in control of themselves—much less their concepts. Society doesn't listen to them anyway. Look into their education and you will find no chain of peace, no capacity for production, and no enjoyed independence; only hatred and a mind schooled in murder. Dogma is their justification, and no one buys theirs except the self-hating bomb bait. There is a special place in Hell reserved for those who don't use their head—who practice what they have known was wrong since they were children.

Their perfect world *is* bombed out cars and buildings—it looks like home to them. The only lasting symbolism they have accomplished and my answer to them is as follows: If you have degenerated to the point where your own death is your most glorious day, odds are high that the world agrees with you. When you destroy pinnacles instead of aspiring to them, when you make claims of Divine intentions yet by example produce only a sea of blood, then you have chosen an obvious side, and our moral road is clear. Ask yourself what you have done that the world can be proud of. As a soldier, ever notice how your dogma directs and trains you to commit atrocities in the name of peace, but never spends any time defining sound living structures of peace, or any civil actions that lead to it? That is because the civilization in America *is* the structure of true, rational, productive peace. The truth is, you are a patsy for killers who are simply more experienced in subversion, and all that keeps them from self-destruction, is *your* destruction. If you want to live, the pattern of *life* is what you must practice. Turn them over and get a job; drop your weapons and join civilization, because the end is coming for your organizations—soon.

Fear-driven Government

"Men and nations behave wisely once they have exhausted all the other alternatives." —Abba Eban

Socialism

There has been a resurgence of this governing concept since the economic collapse; it has grown in popularity with the young as they run from one evil they've seen in practice towards another they haven't, so we need to understand its true nature and result.

Politically, moral subversion takes the form of social systems set up in countries that claim will provide the people with much more wealth than is possible in America, and ends up doing just that—for the politically connected one percent—and slaughters the rest. Whether we are sacrificed to a god or to a State, the result is the same. No matter the benefactor, it is *the sacrifice of life* as a means of survival. Spirit Murderers consider voluntary sacrifice the highest moral gift. Then they omit appreciation and make gift-giving *involuntary*. The hidden intent is to take the moral dilemma out of stealing, but take a look at the nature of a gift. A gift can be given *only* after our sustenance is secured, but they expand the concept to demand everything we have, claiming an even greater joy will be had—not the panic that actually ensues. Having no personal boundaries or rights to anything we create, ultimately pits us all against each other. History records another name for this affront to civility: Socialism, which is just a confused moral cover for slavery. The honorable American system of "payment for services rendered" is *evil* to the Fear-driven as they do not intend to pay. Likewise, they don't ask for payment, because they don't intend to produce anything of value.

Socialism sees a man, whether he is doctor or a janitor, as a human body. The same body gets the same payment, regardless of its contribution. Socialism is a subversive exaltation of the working class, which dissolves all other classes and places the majority of living action under centralized control. Only the top level makes decisions. To them, disagreement is a sickness, ability is a sickness, and punishment is the cure. Their foggy ideals are based on nothing but clever ways to expropriate, as robbers sympathetic to all incapacities split up the production generated by those abler. Its inevitable result is degeneration: a cognitive step four loss to the producer resulting in a change of his pattern, which will no longer produce the bounty expected.

Most imagine a dictatorship as a super state of arms with rigid rules, but it isn't. The rules flow with expediency. *They do whatever they want, whenever they want*—the simple pattern of roving criminality, sanctioned by law. Hedonism never sells, but disguise the slaughter of others through *self*-slaughter and ahhh, now you've got something.

Marxism and The Communist Manifesto

No book has had a greater impact on the Spirit Murderers than the Communist Manifesto by Karl Marx. It permits a zealot to justify every evil he practices but on a *world* scale, so it deserves a short refutation here.

Marx acknowledges human coexistence by the Submission/ Domination Axis alone, splitting mankind into enemy camps—the *bourgeois* (pronounced boorzh-wah) and the *proletariat*—the fascist ruler and the trampled slave. But Americans have no right to use force against each other. No worker is chained to his position *or* to his class; he is free to seek employment elsewhere and free to climb as high as his ambition allows. Marx's whole argument against the West is based on a coercion that doesn't exist.

He condemns free trade, which he considers an affront to "*the numberless indefeasible chartered freedoms*" given by a tyrannical power that claims to handle everything by dictating every aspect of life. His whole argument for Communism is based as well, on human rights that don't exist.

Struggling with civilization, Marx admits that "*narrow-mindedness becomes more and more impossible.*" He condemns productive men for civilizing societies, causing "*the barbarian's intensely obstinate hatred of foreigners to capitulate.*" He goes on to say "*The more openly this despotism proclaims gain to be its end and aim, the more petty, the more hateful and the more embittering it is.*" A Spirit Murderer couldn't have said it more clearly than that. Despotism is rule by force, which of course free trade isn't. The motive of profit is the motive of life, which *his* isn't. He is right: there is nothing more embittering than serving life if *death* is what you want. Marx incites workers to destroy imported goods, smash their own machinery, and set factories ablaze—to restore the conditions of the Middle Ages. He outlines the creation of trade unions to organize *rioting—not* for calm deliberations. He asserts that their mission is to destroy all individual property and any means to acquire or maintain it. A key target of Communism is private property—as for a robber—but don't think it is just the rich they are after; their definition of *bourgeois* is "*...the middle-class owner of property. This person must, indeed, be swept out of the way, and made impossible.*" That's you and I.

Communism intends to destroy families, as he claims all the callous bourgeois parents do is teach children how to survive. Marx sums up by saying they must seize all capital and equipment, then increase rapidly the productive forces he claimed there was too much of. Cleverly, he counsels against small experiments in Socialism as they indicate failure on any greater scale and counsels as well against any peaceful means of change. Reflecting the Koran, nothing less than a total, savage commitment is worthy of the red cause. He exclaims that "*The proletarians have nothing to lose but their chains*", poetic chains that don't actually exist.

If ever there was an economic treatise built purely on a savage tantrum, this is it. His State provides no foundation other than pouncing on what other men have made. There is no economic ideology and no constitution, just a delusional dream of taking control of the world. Sadly enough, by this *supposed* idealism, they have taken half of it, and with every engineered financial panic, they take more. Any hegemonic interest will pursue socialism, as it is simply the consolidation of power. Imagine turning over the nation to the inmates of an asylum, convicted felons, and welfare leaches. What would they declare as legal? Confiscation, rape, racial genocide, random murder, pure loyalty *or else*, and censorship, so that no one could speak against them. The result would be organized looting and wholesale slaughter, benefiting only the most ruthless. They say "*Socialism is the sacrifice of the individual for the benefit of the whole.*" If a cannibal could speak, this would be his argument.

Anti-Biological Pretense

Socialism intends to hold all values static for all men, which is in total contradiction with the flow of life itself, with the biological workings of living organisms, with the weather, you name it. Nothing conforms to a fixed sustenance or a fixed pride for Man except the standards—the axioms they evade. It implies that Man's answer to life and every move must be perfect off the bat, with no variation. But achievement and happiness are had by conscious effort alone, attained individually to the extent of one's ability and application. They are never achieved by random means and can never be granted to all men by law. All the law can do is grant the protection necessary to pursue them.

A dictatorship could never keep up in time or depth with the intricate advancements found in every microcosm of free human endeavor, making an attempt at centralized control even more ludicrous. Yet they sell the illusion that they will provide everything for the populace, and are supported by the mass that fears to face life alone.

Spirit Murderers promote the confusion of *free* meaning uncoerced, with *free* meaning something for nothing. In America *the people* are free, the products aren't, and hence, a massive abundance of products to make life easier. In communist countries, the products are free, the people aren't, and hence, no products and no life. They seize the results and wipe out the causes, and any future bounty as a consequence. Completion of the 1-4 level pattern of survival is made *impossible* by Communism. Look at the United Nation's Bill of Rights. It has thirty articles, where 22, 23, 25 and 29 nullify the rest. The joke is, socialists give men the right to *each other*, which negates all rights.

Once at a car company, I was ushered into a mass gathering about future products along with hundreds of other employees. Walking into the auditorium, I noticed the social contrast: no huge locks on the doors, as in the Dachau concentration camp showers. Listening, I felt no fear; they didn't ask for unquestioning trust, but appealed to our rational minds. We were not segregated by our faith, but brought together for our competence. We were not deceived into our deaths, but voluntarily assembled to earn our livings. *This* is the essence of American Capitalism in action.

The Socialist Utopia

What would life look like if America turned socialist? In a socialist economy, you don't peruse a coffee isle with many brands to choose from; you get a paper sack of dirt and beans with COFFEE written on the side, if at all; and all other products are of the same stale, no-brand quality. Everything is rationed, proportionate to party status. Instead of vast supermarkets and countless choices, there is coffee day, bread day, fish day, lard day, and each time you stand in line for hours—rain, sleet, or snow. Every few weeks the quality drops—the meat more rancid, the lard more spoiled, the bread more stale—and your family's health is deteriorating along with it.

Everything you own is now the property of the State. Soon there is a family living in your basement; then another taking half your home. Then you will be permitted one room, then one corner of the room. Can you complain? Don't dare: they own thought, too. Independent judgment and freedom were American attributes and free trade capitalism was its outgrowth, all thrown away with the bathwater. Now, such an approach to life is banned. As the Bush family motto implies, *"Support us or you are the enemy."* Do you imagine your head still held high in sacrifice for the great communal ideal?

We hear about the drunken parties of those in good standing; we see their red cheeks and healthy skin, while we're all bones and dark circles. We watch our energy being recklessly consumed, whose replenishing consists of a whip on our backs. Express a complaint, let anything slip, and you're dead.

Imagine walking down the street with no right to the contents of your pockets, with even your smallest day-to-day preparations and simplest conveniences thwarted. *Hoarding* they call it. Imagine restraining yourself from showing any sign of ability or even giving an opinion for fear of being enslaved or martyred. This is an example of where all the tenets of Spirit Murder—emergency ethics, sacrifice, selfless servitude, and infirmity worship—align under one institutional structure. It has engulfed half the world's governments, and such premises are responsible for the moral and economic trauma in America as well. All the world's *see and seize* policies from military conquest to welfare, alimony, and unfair taxation are the mongrel cancer of altruist fantasy; the desire of the inept to be powerful, of the ugly to be beautiful, of the sick to be healthy, and to gain it all by devouring those who are.

As ninety-nine percent or more of our lives is not spent in foxholes or running from tornadoes, it should be clear that *sound* moral guidance concentrates on long-range human progress under the conditions that make settled life possible. Morality is concerned with the proper method of producing and accumulating values—*not* with their relinquishment, and mankind's institutions must reflect that. The next time you hear a call for sacrifice, make sure they jump first. It is senseless to claim that men must enter into predicaments where they have no choice but to come out with less; that wars are necessary for technological advances; that people must die for life to go on—this is all the cannibal insanity of an abandoned mind.

Censorship

If socialist dictatorships are so interested in peace, why do they require a purge of every idea which is not theirs? It is the theory that any distrust is disunity—a sickness that must be eradicated in order for the system to survive. Any public interest outside their control is a pressure point to be eliminated. Any other form of power is a threat. Censorship fulfills the promise to destroy families, infusing youth with a drunken sense of power over their own parents. A word whispered against the State—true *or* contrived—will get them hauled away. Parents and contrarian thinkers live in fear, as all loyalties and rational hierarchies are erased in obedience to the State.

Defection

Soviet citizens know that an American living in a slum is wealthier than any inhabitant of a country disallowing free expression. They know—likely by first-hand experience—that poverty is infinitely preferable to the physical and spiritual straight-jacket of Communism, where human beings are reduced to the living-code of ants, unable to use their cognitive tools, tormented by life itself, with no chance to rise.

We have witnessed the horrific defections attempted at any cost from *all* socialist countries, most clearly from East to West Berlin as children were shot in the back while trying to flee. Can any socialist premise be supported when you see its citizens running for their lives? Another way to comprehend the truth and intention of socialist governments is to compare the results by war percentages: the number killed, the number wounded, and the number missing. Socialism shows percentages such as: 20 percent, 50 percent, 10 percent. Capitalism shows percentages such as: .001, .01, and .001, which are a direct result of the American Bill of Rights. So which style of government establishes *true* peace on Earth? Socialism/Communism is efficient only in horror, perhaps destroying five thousand lives to feed five hundred. It is another name for declaring war on one's own people.

Invasion and Immigration

Ask anyone living under a socialist system how many times their family's savings has been wiped out by currency inflation, how often their homes have been ransacked and how many loved ones have been carted away, never to be seen again. In America, we have no emergencies to recover from day after day, and the more sane and less restrictive our social system, the rarer they are to occur. In fact, in civil times, the number of proper sacrificial scenarios is exactly...none. The only screaming heard on U.S. soil, is at our amusement parks.

Free countries hold the moral right to invade and emancipate slave countries when the risks are reasonable. Doing so, their people would no longer need to seek asylum, eliminating immigration problems in the United States. No one wants to leave their homes anyway; some rulers just make it impossible to stay.

Man's greatest weapon against men has always been *altruism*; or *the sacrifice of self to others*. I say to mankind, *"I'll carry you to safety on my back, but don't expect to stay there."* We have many challenges in America, but demolishing our system and abandoning our fundamentals in preference to socialism is not the answer. Personal sovereignty is the hallmark of civilization, *not* voluntary enslavement. We must demolish the organizations that have chosen this fate for us.

Pitchforks, Follow Me...

"[I]t is now too late to retire from the contest. There is no retreat but in submission and slavery! Our chains are forged! ... Gentlemen may cry, Peace, Peace but there is no peace. The war is actually begun! – Patrick Henry

It is confounding and exhaustive to think that there are a million different conspiracies going on and that we have to fight them all: in each and every subject, each and every industry, each and every company, every town, every state... Who has time for that? After working all day, getting the pets fed and walked, getting the kids fed and bathed, we are lucky to have an hour each evening to devote to policing the moral progress of our country. Well, what if there was only one main conspiracy to learn about, manage, and defeat?

What if there was only one core mindset responsible for all of the devastation in the world (the fear-driven), and only six or so such families, *the sick rich,* who control the majority of the world's wealth? Degenerate descendants who own controlling interest or at least large quantities of stock in all of the major companies of the world; banking and finance, military hardware and pharmaceuticals, media and entertainment, home and personal hygiene products, energy and agriculture? Holding large sway in all of them, suddenly all of them stepping to the same tune makes sense. If you work for any of these essential industries and wish to keep your job or career intact, you had better tow the company line. As a reporter, if you think you can blow the whistle and go to another newspaper, you will find yourself blacklisted in minutes with one phone call.

What if, at this level, it was decided that there are too many people on the planet and the majority must die? It would be pretty easy to coordinate an effort to dumb down, sicken, kill, and dispose of us: to repress cures, fill products with complimentary toxins, poison the air and water with toxic nano metals, pollute the soil so nothing could grow except food you have engineered for the polluted environment, spread propaganda as cover, disallow stories to run that expose you, and attack as kooks all those who are investigating.

Imagine being that rich. You could buy any politician. You could fund *both* sides so regardless of who wins, they are indebted to you. Imagine being a politician, stunned to have just received a $200,000 donation and how that would influence your decision in any issue affecting the donor (and we wonder why most politicians are perpetually deaf, dumb, and blind to the obvious good of the people). You feel good because they favored you, but later, you find out that they donated ten times as much to your opponent. Imagine being the corrupt rich; if either side doesn't pay up, the inquisitors in your media arm can quickly destroy them. Is someone becoming a thorn in your side? $50,000 is enough to fund a mercenary to get rid of them; just call General X who runs his special groups to arrange it. Need a cover story too, or to buy a judge? $50,000 more. With our secret militaries operating outside the law's reach, it is like ordering at McDonald's for them.

We need creativity in considering the form and tactics of our enemy because Spirit Murderers have no moral limits, and at this level, unlimited resources. From this height, you can see the twisted logic that drives their choices. They were educated, but they never really needed it like we do. They are not at risk; they don't have to work. And this idleness has driven them insane. What does someone do when they know they can get away with anything? When no thought pattern is linked to life's fundamental preservation? How does this mindset morph over generations? Hitler, Marx, Lincoln, Franklin—prizing conquest over the earned, they envy the historical figures we despise and despise the figures we honor. It should be no surprise that they mimic corrupt leaders who came before them, attempting to actualize their shared vision.

No More Dirty Tricks

"[T]he only thing we have to fear is fear itself– nameless, unreasoning, unjustified terror which paralyzes needed efforts to convert retreat into advance." -Franklin D. Roosevelt

The banking monopoly created our intelligence networks with the goal of unlimited and secret police powers. For example, our Surveillance State doesn't work. We should recognize that if any terrorist acts get through now—real or contrived—(and they have), that mass private data collection is ineffective and its apparatus should be dismantled. Though it lets the corrupt rich spy on their more honorable competitors or anyone who could threaten them (its *true* purpose), it is proof of an unwise investment for the people and only serves to accelerate the consolidation of wealth and control into fewer and fewer hands.

In 1975, CIA Director William Colby admitted under oath that his agents committed over 100,000 major crimes every year. This statistic was repeated in a congressional report in 1996: *"Hundreds of employees on a daily basis are directed to break extremely serious laws... A safe estimate is that several hundred times every day (easily 100,000 times a year) DO officers engage in highly illegal activities."* With the incredible expansion of the Security State and intelligence organizations in America, how many crimes do they commit now? How many news stories of crimes around the world are actually these groups coordinating and committing violent acts to steer public opinion? Don't you think we should know? After the Kennedy assassination and all of the statesman, investigators, and witnesses who have died mysteriously, we have good reason to be paranoid, and should err on the side of caution. What if our secret organizations have chosen *not* to defend us? What if they were never meant to in the first place? To paraphrase Dr. Martin Luther King, *"We've given guided missiles to misguided men."* As a result of the banking cartel-Central Intelligence combination in America, unlimited evil has been unleashed across the planet, yielding such abominations as the Bush dynasty and their life, freedom, and country-destroying Patriot Act. Like cartels exist in all other countries, and they invest together, coordinate attacks together, and reap the rewards of fraud on a scale most cannot conceive of. All secret government organizations must be abolished, and in the meantime, be subject to the moral scrutiny of our Congress and citizen panels.

Our citizens must destroy and completely dismantle the structures of corrupt organized wealth in America. People who are above the law are not worthy of it and deserve no protection under it. They are the proper targets of those who abide by it. We need a body of laws designed specifically against the political encroachment of organized wealth; violations of which will result in the seizure of their assets and lengthy prison terms. Their deadly actions, while always historically reprehensible, are becoming more and more blatant. We endure spectacular displays of fascist dishonor: super PACs, corporations are considered people, we are slaves to debt on money that doesn't exist...It is time to strike; to stabilize our nation and protect it from their further harm. Just look for the head of the snake and cut it off. The rest will work itself out.

So who has time to look?

Whistleblowers and the Anonymous Destruction of Evil

"In the beginning of a change the patriot is a scarce man, and brave, and hated and scorned. When his cause succeeds, the timid join him, for then it costs nothing to be a patriot."
-Mark Twain

We studied whistleblowers in my Master's program. While most observers agreed with them and wanted the truth, the whistleblower did not fare well personally. First of all, they would be fired, and would struggle just to survive after that. Prospective employers were paranoid, fearing that this individual would be looking for something wrong in his or her organization to expose. They were abandoned: coworkers and other industry professionals who had worked hard for their educations, careers, homes, and families didn't want to risk it all by association. Even the whistleblower's family wanted them to play it safe. In most cases, being a whistleblower damaged their lives.

It takes great courage to live by principles rather than by social expediency; you stick your neck out. It takes the same courage to align with someone who has. Most are only comfortable with taking a stand when they see the crowd shifting toward the whistleblower; then they can shuffle over in support and not be singled out. It is basic herd mentality (safe in the herd). The thieving rich know this social mindset intimately. Propaganda is all about controlling mass opinion and mass conduct; that is why controlling the dissemination of news and information is so important; shaping general consensus steers the sheep. We can only act on the information they permit us to have. That is not freedom. If you are afraid—and you have good reason to be—act anonymously, but *act*. When the people see things getting worse and become convinced a new direction is needed, how quickly the tide can change. But for that to come about, we need leaks. Leaks they can't control. So many leaks, their ship sinks.

"One man with courage is a majority" -Thomas Jefferson

We need ways for *The People* to regain power and potency; to not be at risk for investigating and exposing high profile crimes. Further, we need to develop a culture of shrill intolerance for those abusing their positions. Here are a few ideas: Set your career in one field. Choose a crusade in another. Keep these lives separate if possible. Perhaps you can cross-pollinate: speak for another whistleblower or investigative group while you provide expertise to them on corruption in your field. Multiple issues can get addressed while everyone contributes with minimal career and life repercussions.

Carry a gun to protect yourself from the mercenaries hired by the corrupt rich. If your bright future involves cancer research or anything that could have a life-changing impact on the world—especially in billion and trillion dollar industries—you will be a target of the world's worst who are trying to dominate that market and keep the money flowing. Watch your six and shoot back.

We lose American soldiers every day; patriots who give their lives for this great country; for what we believe it to be, for what it was...how can *we* shrink from our responsibility to assure it remains what it can and ought to be? It has come to the point where our lives are precarious, our careers are unstable; we can't plan long range. We can't enjoy the present when we are so worried about the future. We have to risk what we consider our safety in not rocking the boat, because they have already taken our peace of mind.

The Elder Solution

If you are retired, you are in the perfect position to investigate high profile crimes. Your livelihood is not at risk. You have professional credibility and extensive life experience. Most importantly, you have the same amount of time to match what the sick rich dedicate to enslaving us all. Most citizens in their busy middle years do not. Besides, you have lived a full life. If there are any risks to take, it is the right time to take them. And with the mortgage interest shield mentioned earlier, you can pay you house off sooner, retire sooner, and bring more youthful vibrancy to the cause. You should not be sitting idle. With your wide field of view, you deserve to be heard. This could be the most significant part of your life: your vision and legacy.

We don't honor our elders in America as they do in other cultures; we need to change. Aging isn't shameful. It should be recognized as an ascension: a rite of passage. Dismissing our elders and evading our own aging selves by trying to keep up with the latest youth trends is what is shameful. We should stay as youthful and vibrant as long as we can, of course, but aging can and should be a graceful and respected process that grants us greater authority and greater control. We all want to pass down what we have learned, and those who are younger should have reason to look up to us for our knowledge and daily conduct. It doesn't matter how old you are: to stay relevant, all you have to do is stay involved. If you have lost momentum, start it back up: a little more each day and you will recover your potency faster than you ever imagined.

We have this incredible, untapped resource: millions of great minds wasting away in front of televisions and in retirement homes when they could be making a significant impact on the moral direction of our country. They have given us so much and have endured so much to do so; cherish them. Listen to them. Let's get citizens groups run by our respected elders started. Crafts time is over. Save us.

America's Moral Warrior

"Is life so dear, or peace so sweet, as to be purchased at the price of chains and slavery? ... I know not what course others may take; but as for me, give me liberty or give me death!"
– Patrick Henry

We have been through a lot in America; we have suffered staggering blows that have traumatized our nation. Still, I can't help but express immense gratitude to my country and all it has made possible for me to enjoy in my life. It has been a grand adventure, and it doesn't end here. We will rise from the ashes, stronger, wiser and well armed for the challenges and opportunities that await us. The vigilant guardians of life have only to discover their role, and how suitable for it they already are.

I believe most people are decent and do the best they can, and would gravitate naturally toward the path of righteousness if it were only straight and narrow as promised. But what is offered in society today is a moral wilderness, which I hope is now significantly clearer. With a new level of confidence and resolve, we can author a new destiny for mankind. Morality shouldn't require a warrior stance, but at this point in history, it is necessary. The ancient beast has found no resistance in the flinching eyes of its victims. We must reverse this primeval malady and take positive control. It is my mission to restore moral potency in the minds of individual men; to give them, not just a semblance of control over their lives, but *total authority*. The America of the future isn't dependent on one honorable leader emerging; we need a leader in *every* life. As in ballet, the performers must be in shape and know the dance *before* any choreography can be attempted. We would all like to change the world and we can, but it must start with ourselves, and be spread by example. True peace begins *within* every man. Quiet the individual and you quiet the nation. To lift darkness off the Earth, we must first lift it from our own brow.

For those who want to achieve the deepest clarity and reach it quickly, I have developed audio programs for this purpose: *A Bridge Between Us All* (a 4 CD set) is available FREE on I-tunes, and *Sovereignty* (a 12 CD set) can be found at MoralArmor.com or EthicsReloaded.com. With these programs, you will be able to walk through the world with these ideas as a chorus in the background. Once they take, the spiritual rewards are practically beyond description. The incredible sense of personal significance most people feel only once or twice in life, you can come to feel a few times every day—for you and for all those you share it with—and it will keep getting more and more frequent and more and more powerful. Moral hesitation will be gone, and (paraphrasing Ayn Rand) the roads in your life will be as open to achievement as they are to sight. That is the good side...now what about the armor?

Those who reach the point beyond all doubt—the point of total conviction by rational means—those who know the Spirit Murderer's evasions, escapes, and denials; those who learn to answer them in every context and watch them fold in their true impotence, time and time again, become *untouchable* psychologically. With pure honesty, there are no longer any psychological threats to fear. With full willingness to see everything about ourselves and the world, we will have eliminated them. When you can breathe deeply and, with steady eyes, are able to see what is right and wrong and who stands where, no danger is ever too frightening; not even death. You will have become the kind of patriot that America's survival—and peace on Earth for that matter—depends on.

We have all felt from time to time that morality was a steamroller—one with a malevolent driver—endangering everything in its path. Well morality *is* a steamroller, that is true; but with the proper Moral Armor, *we* are behind the wheel. In times of warfare, weapons can be overtaken and used by our opposition. That is what has been done to us for centuries. It is time to turn the tables. No matter what torture I for one have endured or will endure, the damage they can do now is limited. I know what moves them. To gain their acceptance and deflect their animosity requires that we be victims. I refuse to exist as a victim any longer. I refuse to let go of my dreams. I refuse to see the world through the vision of their panic. I refuse to cower to their supernatural threats. I refuse to *just live* with whatever irrational situation they present to us and to consider reform futile. I refuse to feed the rat.

Spirit Murderers have always made the honest, efforting individuals pay for achieving in body and spirit, what *they* betrayed. Now, it is time to fulfill their greatest fear; letting them witness the morally-pure reaching critical mass. We cannot win playing by their rules; the rules must be ours. Evil gains its power only through the life-force that is willing to serve it, and we have a choice in the matter. We are not tied; we are as free as the risks and responsibilities we are willing to assume. Breaking free of their reign requires that you stand and declare what I declared to end my sacrifice: *"If you continue to make me pay for my virtues, they will no longer serve you."*

Peace and civility are not sustained when the public stands down to oppressive forces, but only when sound human rights are respected and fought for, where sole consideration of fostering the life of the individual is held as the key element defining any social order. A Moral Warrior is needed to win a moral war, and this is one. We must learn our enemy well. We must understand the structure of evil and of all that threatens living harmony. We must develop to where we can face our adversaries head on and see *them* cower for once, realizing their age-old fraud is no longer working. *To dominate,* when they see they have lost control of us morally. *To win,* as they roll over in shame and give up their game. Then to come back and teach that they need not fear us—that we will *never* relinquish moral control again, but will be glad to help them face life responsibly and grow, as now they know they must. It will be difficult and painful, but it won't kill them—it will save those who can be saved.

A Brilliant New Destiny for Mankind

"In the long history of the world, only a few generations have been granted the role of defending freedom in its hour of maximum danger. I do not shrink from this responsibility – I welcome it. ... The energy, the faith, the devotion which we bring to this endeavor will light our country and all who serve it. And the glow from that fire can truly light the world."
—John F. Kennedy

The war will be won when pure motives become the world's precedence. We must clear away the wreckage of institutionalized inequities and redesign all that is not consonant with the proper flow of life. If we wish men to live happily on this Earth, we must sanction our own nature and never tolerate its violation.

Let us move into the future with a crystal clear, glistening morality before us; a morality we can all agree on; a morality based on nature itself. As compensation, I want to see looking back at me, not a defiant tension, but a vibrant sense of ease and recaptured innocence: the healthy exhilaration of eyes that *know* what they're winning.

Our Forefathers began their revolution with a Tea Party, and if necessary, so shall we. We win this war when evil is driven underground by the collective acknowledgment of its shame. We win when the highest and best are free to lead, when the rest are free to develop, and the preservation of body and spirit is fostered and respected by all.

Appendix A:

The American Bill of Rights

Amendment 1 - Freedom of Religion, Press, Expression. Congress shall make no law respecting an establishment of religion, or prohibiting the free exercise thereof; or abridging the freedom of speech, or of the press; or the right of the people peaceably to assemble, and to petition the Government for a redress of grievances.

Amendment 2 - Right to Bear Arms. A well-regulated Militia, being necessary to the security of a Free State, the right of the people to keep and bear Arms, shall not be infringed.

Amendment 3 - Quartering of Soldiers. No Soldier shall, in time of peace be quartered in any house, without the consent of the Owner, nor in time of war, but in a manner to be prescribed by law.

Amendment 4 - Search and Seizure. The right of the people to be secure in their persons, houses, papers, and effects, against unreasonable searches and seizures, shall not be violated, and no Warrants shall issue, but upon probable cause, supported by Oath or affirmation, and particularly describing the place to be searched, and the persons or things to be seized.

Amendment 5 - Trial and Punishment, Compensation for Takings. No person shall be held to answer for a capital, or otherwise infamous crime, unless on a presentment or indictment of a Grand Jury, except in cases arising in the land or naval forces, or in the Militia, when in actual service in time of War or public danger; nor shall any person be subject for the same offense to be twice put in jeopardy of life or limb; nor shall be compelled in any criminal case to be a witness against himself, nor be deprived of life, liberty, or property, without due process of law; nor shall private property be taken for public use, without just compensation.

Amendment 6 - Right to Speedy Trial, Confrontation of Witnesses. In all criminal prosecutions, the accused shall enjoy the right to a speedy and public trial, by an impartial jury of the State and district wherein the crime shall have been committed, which district shall have been previously ascertained by law, and to be informed of the nature and cause of the accusation; to be confronted with the witnesses against him; to have compulsory process for obtaining witnesses in his favor, and to have the Assistance of Counsel for his defense.

Amendment 7 - Trial by Jury in Civil Cases. In Suits at common law, where the value in controversy shall exceed twenty dollars, the right of trial by jury shall be preserved, and no fact tried by a jury, shall be otherwise re-examined in any Court of the United States, than according to the rules of the common law.

Amendment 8 - Cruel and Unusual Punishment. Excessive bail shall not be required, nor excessive fines imposed, nor cruel and unusual punishments inflicted.

Amendment 9 - Construction of Constitution. The enumeration in the Constitution, of certain rights, shall not be construed to deny or disparage others retained by the people.

Amendment 10 - Powers of the States and People. The powers not delegated to the United States by the Constitution, nor prohibited by it to the States, are reserved to the States respectively, or to the people.

* * *

Amendment Z – Abolishment of Debt Slavery

Don't forget your free download of the Quick Mortgage Pay Down Method described in Chapter Eight. American freedom is priceless, but your future will be much brighter as an invulnerable, *debt-free* American. Pay your home off fast and save the rest for retirement, your kids, and so that *the people* become the kind of safe, secure, economic force the corrupt rich dread. Whether you are a homeowner or have yet to pursue the American Dream, go to EthicsReloaded.com now and squirrel the file away for the right time.

Appendix B:

Nature's Moral Patterns

The Pattern of Life:

1. Perception
2. Identification
3. Creative Action
4. Reward

We see, we understand, we take action, and we get a result. Most often it is a reward; primarily, *life itself.* This is the moral-biological pattern of survival for Man. If this is the pattern of life, then *any other pattern* will achieve life's opposite.

The Cognitive Frame of Reference for Human Action:

1. Individual
2. Social
3. Artistic
4. Institutional

Concepts must be manageable in thought, so this simple frame of reference allows us to separate and classify all attributes of human action. From individual to social on up, the moral challenge is to assure that each builds on the one before without contradiction.

The Pattern of Social Action:

1. Perception of Entity
2. Identification of Motive
3. Interaction with Entity
4. Result

All social action exists *beyond* our fundamental thought process. Morally, cognition can never be mixed with interaction.

The Fear-driven Pattern of Consciousness:

1. Panic
2. Evasion
3. Destructive/Parasitical Action
4. Penalty

If we are not perceiving, we are in panic; if we are not trying to understand, we are evading; if we are not taking constructive actions, we are being destructive, and the result will be penalties instead of rewards.

To expand on these patterns and explore their application in today's world, join our newsletter, blog, and whatever the tech wizards dream up to keep us connected and effective at our hub site:
EthicsUnderground.com

About the Author

Ronald E. Springer has spent over ten years developing a fully-integrated moral code for Man. Twenty thousand hours went to create the philosophy of *Moral Armor;* tailored for the direct, practical use of sound moral premises in everyday life.

Ron has been a guest on ABC's *The Mitch Albom Show,* FOX News, CBS, and NBC Radio affiliates, including enjoyable interviews with clergymen. Straightforward yet profound, Ron brings humor and lightheartedness to the audience; just what philosophy has been missing.

Ron holds Bachelor's and Master's degrees from Central Michigan University and has done postgraduate work at Harvard. He spends most of his time researching economics, history, philosophy and psychology, looking to bring new clarity and new armor to Mankind.

* * *

To inquire about interviews, available dates for keynotes, consulting for organizations, or bulk orders of this book in print, please email inquiries to: MoralArmor@gmail.com.

The Origin of *Moral Armor*

If you want to pursue a deeper understanding of this philosophy, the original work, *Moral Armor,* is available to order at major booksellers, Amazon.com, and MoralArmor.com.

Moral Armor is just as it sounds: spiritual protection from the irrational, inconsistent and oppressive beliefs intertwined throughout our culture. With new precision, it topples ancient barriers to fulfillment in life and eliminates moral confusion, providing Man with the most potent form of certainty: moral clarity that is everyday useful.

Moral Armor is the summation of over ten years spent filtering crucial world experience through a deeply studied philosophical framework. The result defines explicitly and simply, their true identity, and the psychological motives driving the two sides. Its scope spans from personal motives and relationships to politics and international finance, uncovering how good and evil are extrapolated throughout the full range of human action.

EBook/Softcover: 433 pages, ISBN 1-4184-1866-8

MoralArmor.com Presents

A Bridge Between Us All

Uniting Mankind with *Nature's* Moral Code

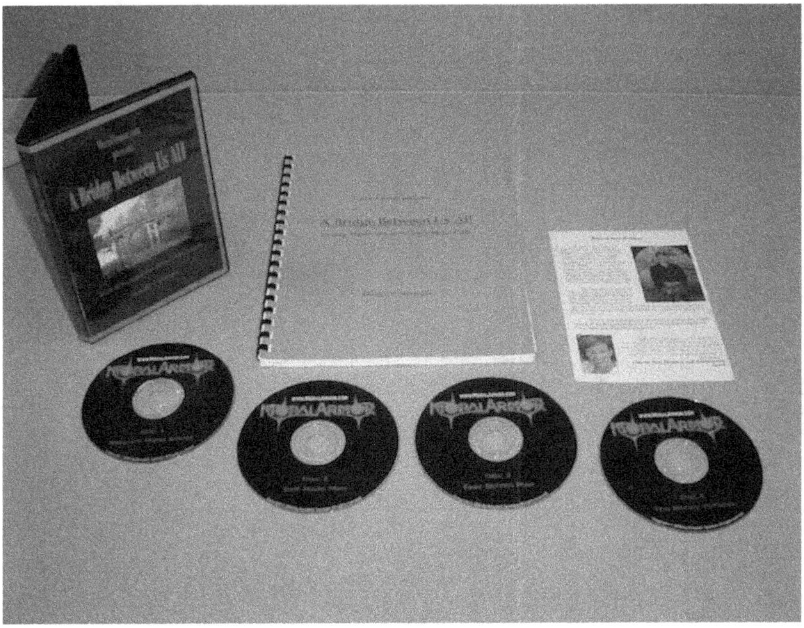

A Bridge Between Us All includes:

1. **4 CD Set:** The most concise description available of *nature's* moral code, showing mankind's like moral intentions clearer than ever before. (4.6 hour running time)
2. 100 page large-print manual.

MoralArmor.com
Presents

Sovereignty

Moral Certainty for Mankind in Four Simple Steps

Moral Armor's flagship audio program *Sovereignty* is our most effective tool. For those who enjoy the ease in repetition of audio learning but still want the most complete understanding, *Sovereignty* offers an in-depth exploration of nature's moral code in 12 CD's. *Sovereignty* takes you by the hand and leads you to the world described in *The Care and Feeding of Freedom*. Take years off your learning curve! (Running time: over 13 hours)

Available at MoralArmor.com and

EthicsReloaded.com

WWW.MORALARMOR.COM

MORALARMOR

MORALITY WAS *MEANT* TO PROTECT YOU!

Join the *Moral Armor* Revolution

"They're guarding all the doors, they're holding all the keys, so sooner or later, someone is going to have to fight them."
—The Matrix

If you feel strongly about the moral and economic restoration of America and want to get involved, join us in arming the nation. We're looking for **Corporate Sponsors, Private Donors, and *Mad Skills*** to aid in expanding mass awareness and driving positive change like never before:

- Funding Media Campaigns
- Making Documentaries
- Hosting Speaking Events, and
- Providing Books to Youth Groups and Non-Profit Organizations
- Internet Exposure and New Tech Wizardry

Individuals can help by leaving a review on Amazon! Sharing it online, and by bringing this opportunity to the attention of the honorable business and charitable organizations you belong to. Email inquiries to:

MoralArmor@gmail.com.

FastDegreeSystems.com presents

Bachelor Monkey!

Swing a Four-Year College Degree in One Year without Going Bananas!

The worst and most hand-wringing frustration in life is not having enough money. Every day, 6,000 more families sink below poverty level. Statistics show that during the economic crisis, the unemployment rate was over 15% for the general population, but only 2% for degreed people. My disdain for school was costly: I was thrown out of work and driven to the brink of starvation along with many others.

With extensive study of my college course bulletin, I found a number of degree accelerating methods which, when put together, turbo-charged the process of getting a degree. The result was that instead of four years or even three, I finished my bachelor's degree in ONE year and three months! I decided to write an eBook outlining exactly what I did so that people anywhere can benefit from the system I developed.

Bachelor Monkey! includes:

- A Quick Start Plan Outlining the Whole Process
- The Fast Lane: How to Choose The Best School for an Accelerated Degree Plan
- Reducing the Cost Per Credit by Up to 5 Times!
- Step-by-Step Instructions for Accumulating Credit at Light Speed
- Staying on Track: Cost and Time Projections for Graduating Fast and Cheap
- How You Can Go to College and Save Your House!
- Simple Instructions to Apply for Financial Aid
- Easy Money: Instructions for the Pell Grant to Save a Fortune You Don't Have to Pay Back!
- Treacherous Traps and School Limitations to Avoid
- Resources Essential to Your Success

Within *Bachelor Monkey!* I chronicle the twists and turns of my whole journey including my mistakes, so you can learn from them (the fact is, I could have graduated even faster). I also outline most of what you will encounter, from financial aid to class scheduling to degree counseling, so you don't have to suffer alone in the fog of a very confusing process.

Even if I'm only half right, you will graduate in two years, still saving several years of your life. Once you're done, I hope you'll say a silent thank you. Something like,

"Thank you so much for sharing this. I'm on the other side now, no longer struggling to stay afloat day after day. My kids have much better lives and I'll save a fortune on their educations, too. My future is secure. My dreams are no longer nightmares. My life is an adventure again. I can breathe again."

Don't wait. Get your copy of *Bachelor Monkey* now. For less than twenty-five bucks, you will save *years*. You will save *thousands*. Your life will never be the same. Afterwards, I'd love to hear your story. Please email and let me know how you did, whom else you've helped, and how your life has changed:

BachelorMonkey@gmail.com

To get started today, swing over to:

BachelorMonkey.com

Dear Reader,

It has been an honor sharing my life's work with you. I hope this journey is just the beginning between us. May we move forward, out of confusion, into immense clarity and elation, and restore our great country to enjoy together for all the generations to come.

Thank you,

Ronald E. Springer

www.ingramcontent.com/pod-product-compliance
Lightning Source LLC
Chambersburg PA
CBHW060835280326
41934CB00007B/798
* 9 7 8 0 9 9 7 6 4 8 3 0 0 *